Sweeter Than Honey

A Devotional Bible Study
on Psalm 119
written by Traci Mae Bergen

ISBN: 979-8-9896216-1-3

Cover and interior design by Traci Bergen
Artwork by Moore & Mountain

Published by Everyday Berean
www.everydayberean.com

Statement of Faith

The Scriptures
- I believe the Bible is the inspired Word of God and the final authority for faith and practice. *(2 Timothy 3:16-17)*
- I believe that God used human authors under the direction of the Holy Spirit to write exactly what He wanted without error or contradiction. *(2 Peter 1:20-21)*

God
- I believe there is only one living and true God, an infinite Spirit, the Creator and Supreme Ruler of heaven and earth. *(Genesis 1:1, Deuteronomy 6:4, Colossians 1:16)*
- I believe that in the unity of the Godhead, there are three persons, the Father, the Son, and the Holy Spirit, who are equal in every divine perfection and work in distinct but harmonious roles. *(1 Corinthians 8:6, 2 Corinthians 13:14, Revelation 4:11)*

Jesus Christ
- I believe Jesus has always existed from the beginning with God. *(John 1:1-3)*
- I believe that the Lord Jesus Christ, the eternal Son of God, became fully human, without ceasing to be God, having been conceived by the Holy Spirit and born of the virgin Mary. *(John 1:1, 2, 14; Luke 1:35; Matt. 1:21-23)*
- I believe that Christ lived a sinless life, died on the cross, and was literally and physically raised from the dead on the third day in order to redeem sinful mankind. *(Romans 3:24-25, Ephesians 1:7, 1 Peter 1:3-5, 1 Peter 2:24, 1 John 3:5)*
- I believe Jesus has ascended to heaven and is now exalted at the right hand of God where, as our High Priest, He acts as our Representative, Intercessor, and Advocate before the Father. *(Acts 1:9-10, Romans 8:34, Hebrews 7:25, Hebrews 9:24, I John 2:1-2)*
- I believe that the Lord Jesus Christ will return again to righteously judge the world at His second coming. *(Mark 14:24-27, Revelation 19:11-16)*

The Holy Spirit
- I believe that the Holy Spirit is a divine person, with God the Father and God the Son, and of the same nature.
- I believe that the Holy Spirit convicts the world of sin, righteousness, and judgment and that He is the supernatural agent in regeneration who baptizes all believers into the body of Christ. *(John 16:8-11, 1 Corinthians 12:13, Titus 3:5)*
- I believe that the Holy Spirit indwells every believer, sealing them for the day of redemption and that He is their abiding Helper, Teacher, and Guide. *(John 14:26, John 16:7, Titus 3:5, Ephesians 1:13-14)*
- I believe the Holy Spirit provides spiritual gifting to each believer for the benefit of the body of Christ. *(1 Corinthians 12)*

Salvation
- I believe salvation only occurs through faith in Jesus Christ. *(John 14:6, Acts 4:12)*
- I believe salvation is the gift of God, not gained by any righteousness of our own, but by grace through faith in Jesus Christ alone. *(Ephesians 2:8-9, Titus 3:4-7)*
- I believe all believers who have genuinely received Christ as their Savior are sealed with the Holy Spirit and are eternally secure in Christ. *(John 6:37-40, John 10:27-30, Romans 8:1, Romans 8:38-39, Ephesians 1:13-14, 1 Peter 1:5)*

i

Introduction

The mission of Everyday Berean is to encourage women to know and love the Word of God in every season. In a culture built on ease, convenience, and immediate gratification, it is vital for us to realize that being a good student of God's Word is not meant to be a quick and easy thing to check off your list. It requires diligence, perseverance, and hard work. The ultimate goal of studying the Scriptures is not to be a "good Christian" or to get all the right answers but to more deeply know the God who has revealed Himself through them. I pray that *Sweeter Than Honey* will be used by the Lord to help you achieve this goal as you spend time with Him through His written Word. This book has been designed to bridge the gap between devotionals and Bible studies. It is perfect for those who are brand new to Bible study, as well as for those who are more seasoned in study but need something lighter for a time.

In the coming days, we will be walking through Psalm 119 together, one stanza at a time. Each day, you will begin by reading a section of the psalm and then answering five questions about the text. Only after you've lightly studied it for yourself will you go on to read a devotional and prayer that I've written about that day's selection of verses. At the end of each day's devotional, there are two application questions to aid you in putting the truths of Psalm 119 into practice in your personal life. There are many reasons why you may be tempted to skip over these, but I encourage you to take the time to prayerfully and honestly answer these questions. This is where the real change happens: not when we gain knowledge of the Scriptures or even of God Himself, but when we let the Holy Spirit *use* that knowledge to make us more like Christ.

I am truly humbled and grateful to get to speak into your life in this way, and I am praying for you as you seek the Lord through Psalm 119. May He stir your affection for the Scriptures and continually open your eyes to behold wondrous things from His instruction.

Cheering you on, friend!

Traci Mae
Founder of Everyday Berean

Study Notes

Key Words & Phrases:

- Keep(ing)/kept
- Meditate
- Delight
- Give me life
- Understand(ing)
- Right(eous)(ness)
- Good
- Hope(d)
- Faithful(ness)
- True/truth
- Love

Other Helpful Information:

Both the date and author of Psalm 119 are unknown, though many scholars attribute this psalm to David based on its style. Some have suggested, based on its content, that he began writing this psalm at a young age and didn't complete it until he was old, making it his life's masterpiece. Whoever the author and whenever this psalm was written, it is indeed a literary masterpiece, having been written in the style of an acrostic. The psalmist follows the order of the twenty-two letters of the Hebrew alphabet, assigning a letter to each stanza and designing each verse within the stanza to begin with that letter.

Day 01

Psalm 119

1. Take a few minutes to read through the entire psalm.

2. Optional notations to make as you read:
- *Names of and references to God*
- *Names or groups of people (e.g. "those whose way is blameless")*

3. Take note of any repeated words or phrases. *I've included a list of key words on the previous page to get you started.*

Psalm 119:1-8

ALEPH

1 Blessed are those whose way is blameless,

  who walk in the law of the Lord!

2 Blessed are those who keep his testimonies,

  who seek him with their whole heart,

3 who also do no wrong,

  but walk in his ways!

4 You have commanded your precepts

  to be kept diligently.

5 Oh that my ways may be steadfast

  in keeping your statutes!

6 Then I shall not be put to shame,

  having my eyes fixed on all your commandments.

7 I will praise you with an upright heart,

  when I learn your righteous rules.

8 I will keep your statutes;

  do not utterly forsake me!

Psalm 119:1-8

NOTES

Day 02

Psalm 119:1-8

1. Who are the people named in verses 1-3?
   - *Those whose way is* _____
   - *Those who walk in* _____
   - *Those who keep* _____
   - *Those who seek* _____
   - *Those who do no* _____
   - *Those who walk in* _____

2. How do the blameless walk (v. 3, 7)?

3. What has the Lord commanded (v. 4)?

4. According to these eight verses, what is the result of obedience to God? Read closely and see how many things you can find.

5. Fill in the following blanks from verses 7-8:
   I will _____ *you with an* _____ *heart,*
   when I _____ *your* _____ *rules.*
   I will _____ *your statutes;*
   do not utterly _____ *me!*
   (Psalm 119:7-8, ESV)

Devotional

The psalmist begins by stating that the person who walks with God is blessed. The Hebrew word used here is *'esher*, which actually means happy. He is not saying that nothing ever goes wrong for them or that those who follow God never feel sadness or grief, but that the state of their soul is blessed in all circumstances. God loves and delights in them (see Proverbs 11:20), and because of this, they have the joy of the Lord holding them steady, whatever comes their way. The writer also adds that those who walk with God don't do anything wrong (v. 3). I think it's important to note that he is not saying this person is perfect or sinless. Rather, they are not making a *practice* of sinning because they are walking with the Lord, who is righteous (see 1 John 3:6-10).

Verse four says that God has commanded His precepts to be kept with diligence. We can take this command with joy because the precepts of the Lord are trustworthy and good, bringing gladness and renewal to our spirits (see Psalm 19:7-11). We see in the psalmist a heart that greatly desires to live a life of integrity, steadfast in obedience to God. His gaze is fixed on God's commands because he knows that adhering to them brings freedom from shame (v. 6). We are given a similar exhortation in the New Testament:

> "And now, little children, abide in him, so that when he appears we may have confidence and not shrink from him in shame at his coming. If you know that he is righteous, you may be sure that everyone who practices righteousness has been born of him."
> 1 John 2:28-29

The psalmist ends this stanza by pleading with the Lord not to forsake him. He knows that God has said He will be found by those who seek Him, but has warned that He will abandon those who abandon Him (see 2 Chronicles 15:2b). In committing to seek the Lord and keep His statues, the psalmist is claiming the blessing and joy of God's presence promised to those who walk according to God's Word.

Application

- **What do your everyday choices look like? Do your actions and responses reveal a faithful and Christlike heart, or are your habits more consistent with your old nature?**

- **Spend some time in prayer, confessing any sinful patterns the Holy Spirit may have brought to your mind just now. Thank Him for the kindness of conviction, and ask Him to grow your love and delight in God's good instruction for His children.**

ALEPH | PRAYER

Heavenly Father,

I pray that I would live a life of obedience to Your instruction and that my heart would be blameless before You.

Keep my heart longing after You, seeking You above all else. Help me not to be distracted by the things of this world but to focus on You so that I can follow Your ways with diligence.

Keep me committed to Your commands, Lord, so that I will not be ashamed but will come to Your Word with a heart full of praise. As I faithfully obey the Scriptures, I see Your righteousness and goodness. I know that You will never leave or forsake me. Thank You for Your presence and Your guidance.

Amen.

Blessed are those who keep his testimonies, who seek him with their *whole heart*

Psalm 119:2

Psalm 119:9–16

BETH

9 How can a young man keep his way pure?

By guarding it according to your word.

10 With my whole heart I seek you;

let me not wander from your commandments!

11 I have stored up your word in my heart,

that I might not sin against you.

12 Blessed are you, O Lord;

teach me your statutes!

13 With my lips I declare

all the rules of your mouth.

14 In the way of your testimonies I delight

as much as in all riches.

15 I will meditate on your precepts

and fix my eyes on your ways.

16 I will delight in your statutes;

I will not forget your word.

Psalm 119:9-16

NOTES

Day 03

Psalm 119:9-16

1. What request is made of the Lord in verse 10?

2. What reason does the psalmist give for storing up God's Word in his heart (v. 11)?

3. What does he ask the Lord to do in verse 12?

4. Does the word "blessed" in verse 12 have the same meaning as "blessed" in verses 1-2? Why or why not? *Hint: this is a good opportunity to look up the original Hebrew words if you have the ability. (BlueLetterBible.org and the Literal Word app are both helpful free tools for this!)*

5. In the space below, write the "I will" statements made in verses 15-16:

Devotional

Verse 9 begins, "How can a young man keep his way pure?"
The writer then answers his own question: "By guarding it according to your word."

The Hebrew word translated as "guarding" here is *shâmar*, and it carries the idea of protecting, carefully watching over, and even placing a hedge around something. The next two verses give us a picture of what this practically looks like.

In verse 10, the psalmist says that he has sought the Lord with all his heart. He has previously said that those who seek the Lord are happy (v. 2), yet he still feels the pull of his flesh. He knows how prone his heart is to wander and cries out to God for help. Verse 11 tells us that treasuring God's Word guards us against sin. If we are truly worshiping God—placing a higher value on Him than all else—we will treasure His Word as a result. Obedience becomes less about puffing ourselves up with knowledge or following a list of rules and more about pleasing the One who means more to us than anything else. The psalmist did not store up the Scriptures only as head knowledge. He kept it in his heart like Mary (see Luke 2:19, 51) and wielded it as a sword, answering temptation in the same way as Jesus Himself (see Matthew 4:1-11). The one who desires to keep his way pure must be proactive, placing a hedge around his heart to guard against anything that might turn his affection from the Lord. He will be continually looking to the Lord for instruction (v. 12), comparing his life to God's Word and adjusting accordingly.

Some of this psalm's themes also begin to emerge in this section. The writer shows a heart that desires to continually learn more of God's instruction and teach it to others.

The psalmist says in verses 14-15 that he delights in the instruction of the Lord and that he will fix his eyes on God's ways. He began this section by asking how he could keep his way pure, and now we see him surrendering his way to God's. He is learning that the wisdom revealed by the Scriptures is of greater value than any earthly treasure because it holds eternal wealth (see Proverbs 8:10-11, 18-19).

The writer of this psalm ends this section by saying that he will meditate on God's Word and will not forget it. I think of the Lord's instruction to Joshua as he prepared to take the place of Moses as leader of the Israelites:

> "This Book of the Law shall not depart from your mouth, but you shall meditate on it day and night, so that you may be careful to do according to all that is written in it. For then you will make your way prosperous, and then you will have good success."
> Joshua 1:8

Meditating on the Scriptures not only helps us remember them but enables us to walk in obedience to God. In this way, the Holy Spirit sanctifies us as we guard our way according to God's Word (v. 9).

Application

- Are you proactively guarding your way, asking the Lord to search you and reveal any grievous way in your heart (see Psalm 139:23-24)? Or do you only confess and repent as you encounter the consequences of your sin?

- Do you meditate on the Scriptures throughout your days, letting them renew your mind and guide your steps? Or do you check off your Bible reading and move on to the next thing without giving the words you read a second thought?

BETH | PRAYER

Lord,

My heart is so prone to wandering from You. Help me to seek You above all else. Help me guard my thoughts, beliefs, and actions and direct my life according to what You have said in Your Word.

Help me treasure Your Word so that I will turn from my sinful desires and delight in obeying You, as You hold the highest value in my heart.

I am so grateful for the wisdom that You offer through the Scriptures. I want to learn more from Your Word each day so that I can reflect You more clearly and proclaim Your truth to those around me. Help me to meditate on, think about, delight in, and remember Your Word. I pray that I would not just receive it as head knowledge but that I would let it change my heart.

Amen.

Psalm 119:17-24

GIMEL

17 Deal bountifully with your servant,

that I may live and keep your word.

18 Open my eyes, that I may behold

wondrous things out of your law.

19 I am a sojourner on the earth;

hide not your commandments from me!

20 My soul is consumed with longing

for your rules at all times.

21 You rebuke the insolent, accursed ones,

who wander from your commandments.

22 Take away from me scorn and contempt,

for I have kept your testimonies.

23 Even though princes sit plotting against me,

your servant will meditate on your statutes.

24 Your testimonies are my delight;

they are my counselors.

Psalm 119:17-24

NOTES

Day 04

Psalm 119:17-24

1. What requests does the psalmist make of the Lord in this section?

2. How does the psalmist refer to himself in verse 19?

3. What does the psalmist say he is consumed with (v. 20)?

4. Who does God rebuke, and why (v. 21)?

5. The Hebrew word translated as "counselors" in verse 24 is ʿēṣâ, and similar to our English definition of counselor, it means one who gives advice or guidance. In the Old Testament, this word is especially used in reference to the counsel and purpose of God.[1] How does this deepen your understanding of this verse?

---

1. "H6098 - ʿēṣâ - Strong's Hebrew Lexicon (ESV)." Blue Letter Bible. Accessed 9 Apr, 2024. https://www.blueletterbible.org/lexicon/h6098/esv/wlc/0-1/

Devotional

This section of Psalm 119 contains several requests from the psalmist to God. They all come back to his core desire to know the Lord more deeply by understanding and obeying His Word. Verse 20 says he is overcome or consumed with longing for God's Word; he is obsessed. He can't stop thinking about it and finds himself continually pondering the Scriptures. We can assume that this psalmist knew God's instruction well, yet he repeatedly asked God to open his eyes and heart to their truths. He knew that God was the source of all knowledge and understanding. He recognized his inability to behold wondrous things from God's Word apart from the wisdom of the Holy Spirit.

In verse 21, the psalmist says that God rebukes those who are cursed because of their arrogance in wandering from God. This hearkens back to Deuteronomy 27, where the people heard the Law clearly stated to them and wholeheartedly agreed to the dire consequences that would come upon them if they turned from it.

In verse 22 of Psalm 119, the writer asks God to remove insults and contempt from him because he has been obedient to God's commands, in contrast to the arrogant and rebellious. This psalmist is facing ridicule for his faithfulness to God (see v. 51), and it feels unfair because those who keep God's Word are supposed to be blessed (see vv. 1-2).

But this is the way of Christ. He walked in perfect obedience to the Father during His earthly life, yet He faced mockery, scorn, and physical suffering, even to the point of death on a cross (see Philippians 2:8). As His followers, we are called to share in His sufferings during our time on this earth, but we can be confident that none of this can separate us from His love (see Romans 8:31-39). We should not be surprised when we face persecution or suffering for the sake of our Savior. Instead of feeling frustrated when we're ridiculed for our faith, we can actually *rejoice*, knowing that we are blessed because the Spirit of glory and of God rests on us (see 1 Peter 4:12-19)!

In the same way, the writer of this psalm commits to remain faithful to God and His Word regardless of the persecution he is receiving. But as we have seen, he knows he cannot keep the law by his own strength. He sees his great need for the Lord's grace to enable him to live in obedience. Like Paul, he truly delights in God's law with his whole being, but his sin nature is continually waging war against him (see Romans 7:22-25). In response, he turns to the only One who can truly help. He looks to the decrees of God for counsel because it is only in the eternal, omniscient One that true wisdom is found.

Application

- Does it surprise you when you are ridiculed or rejected for claiming Christ? Remember that Jesus Himself said we will suffer in this world, but in the same breath, He also said that we can be courageous because He has already won (see John 16:33)! Take a moment to thank God that in Christ our victory is sure and ask Him for steadfastness and courage to stand firm in the truth.

- Think about those you turn to when you need counsel. Is their advice rooted in Scripture or the wisdom of this world?

GIMEL | PRAYER

Heavenly Father,

The pull of my sin nature is so strong; be gracious to me as I seek to follow You. Thank You that my High Priest can sympathize with my weaknesses and that I can boldly come to You for grace when I need help (see Hebrews 4:14-16).

During my time here on earth, I want to be continually learning more of You. I ask that You open my mind and heart to understand the Scriptures, for all wisdom and knowledge come from You, the One who knows all things.

Help me to remain steadfast in the face of suffering, looking to Christ's example and entrusting myself to my faithful Creator, knowing that Your name is glorified through my obedience (see 1 Peter 4:12-19).

Amen.

Psalm 119:25-32

DALETH

25 My soul clings to the dust;

   give me life according to your word!

26 When I told of my ways, you answered me;

   teach me your statutes!

27 Make me understand the way of your precepts,

   and I will meditate on your wondrous works.

28 My soul melts away for sorrow;

   strengthen me according to your word!

29 Put false ways far from me

   and graciously teach me your law!

30 I have chosen the way of faithfulness;

   I set your rules before me.

31 I cling to your testimonies, O Lord;

   let me not be put to shame!

32 I will run in the way of your commandments

   when you enlarge my heart!

Psalm 119:25-32

NOTES

Day 05

Psalm 119:25-32

1. What does the psalmist ask the Lord to do in verse 25? *We will see variations of this request repeated several times throughout the remainder of Psalm 119; consider choosing a specific color or symbol to mark this phrase as you study.*

2. What phrase is repeated in verses 26 and 29?

3. Where does the psalmist look for strength (v. 28)?

4. What does the psalmist say he has chosen (v. 30)?

5. What does the writer of this psalm say the Lord will do or has done for him (v. 32b)? *(This phrase varies quite a bit between translations.)*

Devotional

In this section, we are given a picture of one who is weary and worn down by grief. In the time and culture in which this psalm was written, it was a common outward expression of mourning to throw dust on one's head and sit in ashes. In saying that his soul "clings to the dust" (v. 25), the psalmist conveys that he feels so powerless to rise above his grief that these symbols of suffering have become embedded into his very soul. Yet he knows where his help comes from. He turns to the Lord to revive his spirit and renew his strength in his deep weariness and sorrow. He displays profound humility and dependence on the Lord, admitting his need for help before Him in prayer. As the psalmist can't just pull himself up by his bootstraps and muster up restored joy or a renewed spirit, so neither can we. God alone is the giver of all life and true joy.

He recognizes that without the Lord imparting wisdom to him, he will never understand the Scriptures. Because of this, he asks God Himself to teach him and enlarge his understanding. He is confident that the Lord will hear and answer as he commits his way to Him in prayer. But notice verse 27. The phrasing varies a bit between translations, but the basic idea is the same: the psalmist asks for understanding *so that* he can meditate on the wondrous things found in the Lord's instruction (see v. 18). This is the beauty of the Scriptures. The more we learn of them, the more we love them and will continually ponder their instruction. The Word of God is wondrous because in it, we find the Wondrous One, and the more we understand, the greater awe we will have of Him and all He has said and done!

After considering the great wonders of the Lord, the psalmist circles back to his own weakness and sorrow (v. 28). The phrase translated as "melts away" could also be translated as "collapse" or "crumple."[2] The writer is saying that he is spent; he has no strength left in himself. But again, we see that he knows where to turn for strength. He lifts his gaze to the only One who never grows weary, trusting that He will sustain him (see Isaiah 40:28-29).

In verse 29, the writer asks God to put false ways far from him. Other versions translate this as a request for God to keep or remove him from the way of deceit. Throughout the Bible, words like *path* and *way* are used to refer to one's practice or lifestyle, and this verse is no different. Our psalmist is asking the Lord to teach him His law so that he can walk in faithfulness by committing himself to God's good rules (v. 30). As we will continue to see, despite his great love of the Lord, he is still battling his sinful nature. It is clear throughout this psalm that his weapon of choice is the Scriptures. He fights temptation and practices integrity by keeping God's Word front and center in his mind and heart. As the Lord graciously grants him an understanding of the Scriptures, this leads to a desire to run the race set before him with wholehearted obedience, chasing after the wisdom of God. He clings to God's commands even as his soul clings to the dust, trusting that those who look to the Lord will never be ashamed (see Psalm 34:5).

Application

- **When you are worn down or depressed, how do you typically try to revive yourself or restore your joy? Is your practice self-focused or God-focused?**

- **What do you cling to when you collapse in weariness or grief? Choose 3-5 key Scriptures to memorize that will help you lift your gaze when you're tempted to despair.** *If you're unsure where to begin, start by paying attention during your regular Bible reading. Note any verses stating specific truths about God, and consider adding them to your list!*

2. *NET Bible, Full Notes Edition* (Nashville, TN: Thomas Nelson, 2019), page 1040.

DALETH | PRAYER

Lord,

This life can be overwhelming, and I feel weary so often. I am so grateful to know that my God never grows tired or weary. Renew my strength as I wait for You today.

I love You, Lord, and I long to obey Your good commands, but I need Your help. Open my heart to Your truth and give me wisdom to apply it to my life so that I may walk in faithfulness before You.

Help me to cling to Your Word, keeping my eyes fixed on You and my mind set on things above.

Amen.

Make me understand
the way of your precepts,
and I will meditate
on your *wondrous works.*

Psalm 119:27

Psalm 119:33-40

HE

33 Teach me, O Lord, the way of your statutes;

and I will keep it to the end.

34 Give me understanding, that I may keep your law

and observe it with my whole heart.

35 Lead me in the path of your commandments,

for I delight in it.

36 Incline my heart to your testimonies,

and not to selfish gain!

37 Turn my eyes from looking at worthless things;

and give me life in your ways.

38 Confirm to your servant your promise,

that you may be feared.

39 Turn away the reproach that I dread,

for your rules are good.

40 Behold, I long for your precepts;

in your righteousness give me life!

Psalm 119:33-40

NOTES

Day 06

Psalm 119:33-40

1. For what reason does the psalmist ask for understanding (vv. 33-34)?

2. What does the psalmist ask God to turn his heart to (v. 36)?

3. From what does he ask the Lord to turn his eyes away (v. 37)?

4. How does the psalmist describe the Lord's rules in verse 39?

5. In what does he look for life (v. 40)?

Devotional

When someone asks us to do something, we might agree depending on who it is or how well we know them. But when we understand *why* we are doing something, our actions are wholehearted and purposeful. We should obey the Lord because He is good and trustworthy (and, quite simply, because He is God), but it is much easier to walk in wholehearted obedience when we understand the reasoning behind His instructions. In this section of the psalm, the writer continues to ask God to teach him, and in verses 33-34, he asks for understanding specifically for the purpose of keeping His commandments.

The Hebrew word translated as "understanding" in verse 34 is *bîn*, and it carries the meaning of understanding by distinguishing or discerning.[3] It appears often throughout this entire psalm because this is an intense longing of the psalmist's heart. He deeply delights in the Scriptures and is fervently seeking the Lord for the wisdom and discernment needed to follow the path of obedience. We have the same need, for we cannot fully understand God's Word without discerning the correct interpretation of it. Gratefully we know that God will give us wisdom when we ask Him for it, and He will do so generously and without reproach (see James 1:5).

In verse 36, the psalmist asks the Lord to incline his heart to His testimonies.

---

3. "H995 - bîn - Strong's Hebrew Lexicon (ESV)." Blue Letter Bible. Accessed 23 Apr, 2024. https://www.blueletterbible.org/lexicon/h995/esv/wlc/0-1/

The word "incline" here is translated from the Hebrew word *nāṭâ*, and it means to extend, bend, or turn.[4] If someone is inclined to something, they are drawn to it or lean in its direction; they are *bent* toward that thing. The psalmist poses this heart posture in contrast to that of selfish gain. In the next verse, he prays that he would turn his eyes away from what is worthless and set them instead on the ways of God. Through these requests, we can see that the heart of this psalmist is to selflessly obey the Lord, valuing the eternal above any earthly prosperity or success. We are given a similar exhortation in the New Testament:

> "So if you have been raised with Christ, seek the things above, where Christ is, seated at the right hand of God. Set your minds on things above, not on earthly things."
> Colossians 3:1-2

The last verse in today's selection brings this stanza and the previous one (verses 25-40) full circle. The psalmist asks God to give him life three times in this small section: through His Word (v. 25), through His ways (v. 37), and through His righteousness (v. 40). Clearly, he is not asking God to keep him physically alive; this word holds a moral aspect to it. In the New Testament, the concept of "life" is taken a step further, referring to *eternal* life, which is obtained by obeying God's commands. As sinful humans, we are wholly unable to keep the law perfectly. But we have been offered the gift of eternal life through the One who lived in perfect obedience, and He graciously covers us with *His* righteousness. This prayer of the psalmist has been answered more fully than he could ever have imagined, as we obtain true life through the very Word and righteousness of God: Jesus Christ Himself (see John 1:1; 5:24-26).

Application

- **When you seek to understand the Bible better, is it simply for the sake of gaining more knowledge or to live in greater obedience?**

- **To what is your heart inclined? Selfish and empty pursuits, or higher, eternal things?**

---

4. "H5186 - nāṭâ - Strong's Hebrew Lexicon (ESV)." Blue Letter Bible. Accessed 23 Apr, 2024. https://www.blueletterbible.org/lexicon/h5186/esv/wlc/0-1/

HE | PRAYER

God,

I want to obey Your instructions, but I need Your help to understand what I read in Your Word. Open my heart and give me wisdom to understand and apply Your truth to my life so that I will walk in wholehearted obedience to You.

Help me truly to delight in You and Your good commandments. Incline my heart to things above rather than my own earthly desires and comforts.

Thank You for the abundant life that I have been given in Christ. May I glorify Your name with my time on this earth, but also remember that this is not my home. Help me to keep my eyes fixed on You.

Amen.

Lead me in the path of
your commandments,
for I *delight* in it.
Psalm 119:35

Psalm 119:41-48

WAW

41 Let your steadfast love come to me, O Lord,

your salvation according to your promise;

42 then shall I have an answer for him who taunts me,

for I trust in your word.

43 And take not the word of truth

utterly out of my mouth,

for my hope is in your rules.

44 I will keep your law continually,

forever and ever,

45 and I shall walk in a wide place,

for I have sought your precepts.

46 I will also speak of your testimonies before kings

and shall not be put to shame,

47 for I find my delight in your commandments,

which I love.

48 I will lift up my hands toward your commandments,

which I love,

and I will meditate on your statutes.

Psalm 119:41-48

NOTES

Day 07

Psalm 119:41-48

1. In verse 41, what two things do the psalmist indicate were promised to him?

2. In what does the psalmist put his hope (v. 43)?

3. What are the four "I will" statements made by the psalmist in this stanza (v. 44, 46, 48)?
- I will _____
- I will _____
- I will _____
- I will _____

4. Where does the psalmist say he will walk because of his obedience to the Lord (v. 45)?

5. What phrase is repeated in verses 47-48?

Devotional

When the Lord brought Israel out of Egypt and gave them the law, He called Himself "the faithful God who keeps covenant and steadfast love with those who love him and keep his commandments" (see Deuteronomy 7:9). Note that this promise hinges upon two things: loving God and keeping His commandments. In our text today, the psalmist calls upon these promises, asking God to show him steadfast love and save him *according to His promise*. He can pray this with confidence as he knows he is living in accord with the law of God, and he serves a God who always keeps His promises. As his prayer is answered, those who taunt him for trusting in the Lord will see that God is faithful, and this psalmist's hope was not in vain. The incomparable reward of obedience puts any voice of ridicule to shame.

The psalmist then asks God to help him boldly speak the truth of the Scriptures. He knows that his hope is not in anything temporary but in the eternal and unchanging Word of God, and it is on this that he resolves to think and speak of all his days. The one who trusts in the Lord speaks freely of His truth without shame or fear of what others think. The hope of the psalmist is not in the praise or admiration of men but in the Lord! He is resolved to keep God's instruction throughout his life because he knows that obedience to a good God is not oppressive or burdensome. Too often, we think of obedience as restrictive, but the psalmist says it enables him to walk "in a wide place" (v. 45). The NASB translates this phrase as "I will walk at liberty." The Hebrew word used here is *rāhāb*, which means "roomy, in any direction, literally or figuratively; broad, large, at liberty."[5] Because God is both our Creator and a good Father, He knows exactly what we need and what is best for us, and His instructions reflect this. Walking in obedience to His Word gives us the freedom to thrive as we live the way for which He created us. Fully convinced of this truth, our psalmist can speak without shame before even the most powerful people. He knows that how he lives matches his spoken testimony, and his convictions are unwavering regardless of whether he is speaking to a humble friend or a powerful king.

All of this is ultimately rooted in his delight in the Scriptures. As he continually dwells on the instruction and wisdom given by the Lord, it brings a welcome change to his heart, driving him to obey. You can outwardly conform to another's desires or instructions, but all genuine obedience begins in the heart. A life that truly exemplifies God's Word is the overflow of a heart that loves and meditates on it.

Application

- A wise friend once told me that we are always meditating on something, so we must be intentional with what we're allowing our minds to dwell on. Look up Philippians 4:8, and take a moment to evaluate your thought life. Confess any untrue, impure, or unlovely thoughts. Then ask the Lord to help you "think on these things"—to meditate on the truth of the Scriptures, just as the writer of Psalm 119.

- Do you obey out of genuine love for the Lord and delight in His Word, or do you follow what the Bible says just because that's what "good" Christians do?

---

5. "H7342 - rāhāb - Strong's Hebrew Lexicon (ESV)." Blue Letter Bible. Accessed 21 May, 2024. https://www.blueletterbible.org/lexicon/h7342/esv/wlc/0-1/

WAW | PRAYER

Heavenly Father,

I praise You. Your salvation is such an unspeakable gift, and Your steadfast love is woven through each of my days. I know that You are faithful, even when I cannot see Your hand at work. Help me to put my hope in You alone, that I would fear You more than I fear what others might think.

You are a good and wise Father, and You only give good commands. Help me to trust that Your commands are not restricting my soul, but putting it at liberty, for freedom from sin and shame is the only true freedom.

Help me to keep Your Word and to speak of its truth with confidence before anyone I come into contact with. I love You, Lord, and I love Your good instruction. Help me to keep You at the center of my pondering, thinking on that which is true, honorable, just, pure, lovely, commendable, excellent, and praiseworthy.

Amen.

I shall walk in
a wide place
for I have
sought your precepts.
Psalm 119:45

37

Psalm 119:49–56

ZAYIN

49 Remember your word to your servant,

    in which you have made me hope.

50 This is my comfort in my affliction,

    that your promise gives me life.

51 The insolent utterly deride me,

    but I do not turn away from your law.

52 When I think of your rules from of old,

    I take comfort, O Lord.

53 Hot indignation seizes me because of the wicked,

    who forsake your law.

54 Your statutes have been my songs

    in the house of my sojourning.

55 I remember your name in the night, O Lord,

    and keep your law.

56 This blessing has fallen to me,

    that I have kept your precepts.

Psalm 119:49-56

NOTES

Day 08

Psalm 119:49-56

1. What does the psalmist ask God to do in verse 49?

2. In what does the psalmist find comfort (v. 50, 52)?

3. What causes him to feel angry (v. 53)?

4. In the night, what does the psalmist remember (v. 55)? Look up Psalm 42:8 for additional insight, and make note of anything helpful.

5. In the ESV, verse 56 begins, "This blessing has fallen to me." Other versions translate this phrase as "This is my practice." Whatever translation you are using, there should be much less variation in the second half of the verse. What does the psalmist describe here as his blessing or practice?

Devotional

Here we see the psalmist continue to stake his hope in God's Word. He begins this stanza by asking the Lord to remember His word. Throughout the Old Testament, when this word is used, it means more than just to think of something; God uses it when He is ready to act. We see Him *remember* people that He loved, like Noah, Abraham, Rachel, and Hannah. He *remembered* the covenants He had made with His people. In each instance, the Lord's remembering is directly connected to an action. The psalmist here is asking the Lord not just to think of him but to *act* on his behalf.

As he waits for the Lord, our psalmist is not without comfort in his affliction. Twice in the first few verses of this section, the psalmist says he takes comfort in the Scriptures. In the second mention, he specifically calls them "your rules from of old" (v. 52). People often claim the Bible to be archaic and irrelevant to us today. Here the psalmist himself calls the Scriptures old, many of them

40

having been written hundreds of years before he was born. Yet it is in these writings of old that he finds instruction *and comfort* because God's truth stands the test of time. What we have already seen the Word of God do, we can trust it to continue to do. This hope in the faithfulness of God to do what He has said is our comfort even in the very midst of suffering.

> "For whatever was written in the past was written for our instruction, so that we may have hope through endurance and through the encouragement from the Scriptures."
> Romans 15:4

The psalmist goes on to say that he feels indignant toward the wicked. This is not because of what they have done to him, though they have surely done enough to warrant anger, as he is regularly derided for his faithfulness to the Lord. He is enraged by the wicked because of their disregard for God and His law. Yet the psalmist remembers that he is but a sojourner on his way to be with the One who is the theme of his songs. In the meantime, he continues to praise the Lord and practice obedience to His Word. His obedience is rooted in a deep and abiding trust that regardless of how foolish it may look to others, God's rules are for our good.

There are varying opinions as to whether the "night" spoken of in verse 55 is literal or figurative. If the psalmist is speaking literally, it would allude more to the things we dwell on when we're alone, in the dark of night. If figurative, this speaks volumes to us about the power of remembering the Lord's goodness and faithfulness during instability, adversity, and suffering. Regardless of which view you take, I think the basic application is the same: the things that we think about God when we are alone reveal the true state of our heart toward Him. As Charles Spurgeon put it,

> "If we do not think of [God] secretly we shall not obey him openly."[6]

It can be easy to see following God's instructions as a burden, but the psalmist views obedience as a blessing! If we know that God is good and, therefore, His rules are good, we can know that obedience to our good and kind God is not burdensome. When we love the Lord with all our heart, soul, mind, and strength, it becomes a joy to do whatever pleases the One we love most.

Application

- When you are in need of comfort, is spending time with the Lord your first instinct or more of a last resort? Consider keeping a list of verses or passages you can draw comfort from and use to encourage others during seasons of suffering.

- Does obedience to God bring you joy or make you feel weighed down? If following His commands feels burdensome, search your heart to see why it may feel that way. Take some time to confess anything the Holy Spirit reveals to you that you're loving more than Him.

---

6. Spurgeon, C. "Psalm 119 Verses 49-56 by C. H. Spurgeon." Blue Letter Bible. Last Modified 5 Dec 2016. https://www.blueletterbible.org/Comm/spurgeon_charles/tod/ps119_049-056.cfm

ZAYIN | PRAYER

Heavenly Father,

I choose to trust today that You are who You say You are and that You will always do what You have said. Your faithfulness is such a great comfort to me in the midst of every uncertainty. Thank You so much for recording Your Word for us "so that we may have hope through endurance and through the encouragement from the Scriptures" (Romans 15:4).

Make Your name the song that is forever in my mouth as I walk in the blessing of obedience to Your good instruction.

Amen.

42

Your statutes have been *my songs* in the house of my sojourning.

Psalm 119:54

43

Day 09

Psalm 119

1. Take a few minutes to read through the entire psalm.

2. Optional notations to make as you read:
   - *Transition or connecting words (so that, because, but, therefore, if/then statements, etc.)*

3. Take note of any repeated words or phrases.

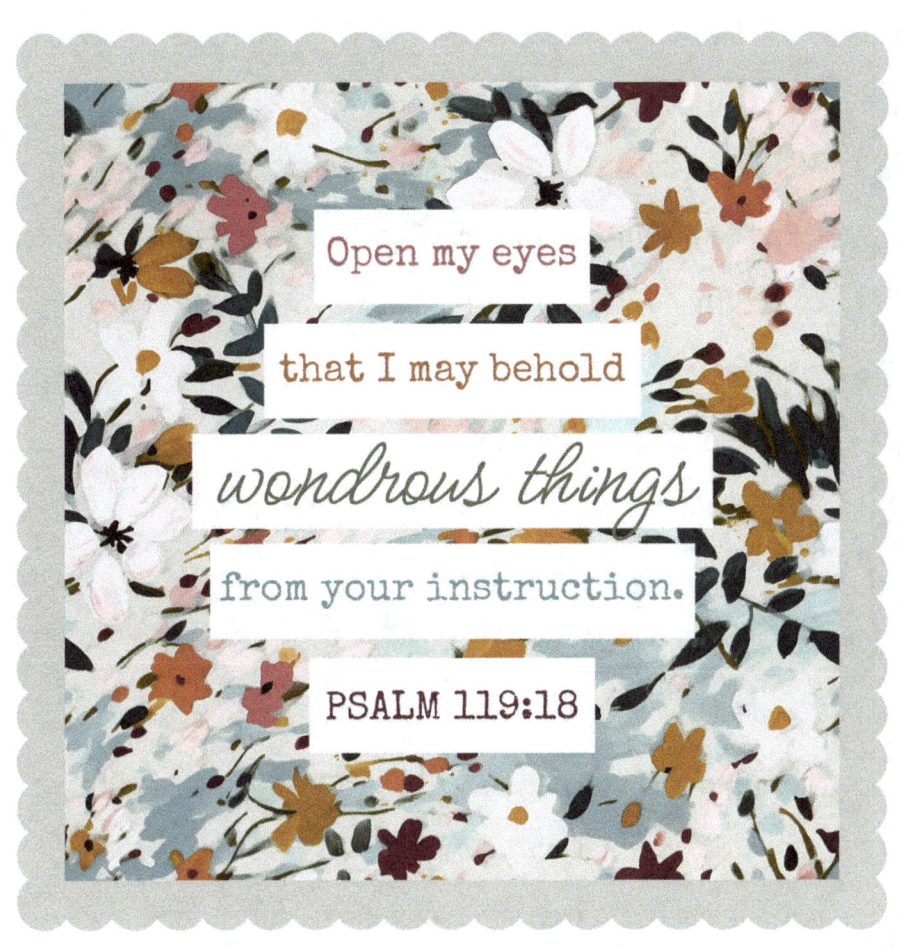

Open my eyes

that I may behold

wondrous things

from your instruction.

PSALM 119:18

Psalm 119:57-64

HETH

57 The Lord is my portion;

    I promise to keep your words.

58 I entreat your favor with all my heart;

    be gracious to me according to your promise.

59 When I think on my ways,

    I turn my feet to your testimonies;

60 I hasten and do not delay

    to keep your commandments.

61 Though the cords of the wicked ensnare me,

    I do not forget your law.

62 At midnight I rise to praise you,

    because of your righteous rules.

63 I am a companion of all who fear you,

    of those who keep your precepts.

64 The earth, O Lord, is full of your steadfast love;

    teach me your statutes!

Psalm 119:57-64

NOTES

Day 10

Psalm 119:57-64

1. What does the psalmist call the Lord in verse 57? What does this mean?

2. What promise does he make to God (v. 57b)?

3. Fill in the following blanks from verses 59-60:
   "When I think on _____ _____,
   I turn my feet to _____ _____;
   I _____ and do not _____
   to _____ your commandments."
   (Psalm 119:59-60, ESV)

4. What time of day does the psalmist praise the Lord (v. 62)?

5. With whom does the psalmist find friendship (v. 63)?

Devotional

This stanza begins with the beautiful statement, "The Lord is my portion." This Hebrew word, ḥēleq, most often refers to one's inheritance or reward. One Bible dictionary states that words translated as "portion" can also refer to something dear and close to a person.[7] Israel is actually called the portion of the Lord (see Deut. 32:9). Yahweh is likewise Israel's portion or inheritance: their ultimate prize. Whichever definition you go with, the idea in this verse is to value the Lord above all else, choosing Him above any earthly goods or riches. If the Lord is your portion, in any and every situation, you will joyfully be able to say, "I'd rather have Jesus." Because the Lord is his portion, the psalmist is committed to obedience. Due to his deep love for and satisfaction

7. *Eerdmans Dictionary of the Bible*, ed. David Noel Freedman, s.v. "portion," (Grand Rapids, MI: Wm. B. Eerdmans Publishing Co., 2000).

in the Lord, he knows there is nothing greater to gain by straying from God's commands, no better way than the one He has set before him.

The psalmist knows that the Lord's favor is on those who seek Him wholeheartedly, so he makes the connection that to seek the Lord is to seek His favor. In asking for favor according to God's promises, he is not expecting earthly prosperity or a trouble-free life. You'll remember that God has promised steadfast love and salvation to those who seek Him (see Ps. 119:41, or Day 7). Our psalmist is simply praying in alignment with God's revealed will: to know His steadfast love more deeply and to love Him more deeply in return.

Of course, he is still learning obedience like the rest of us. In verse 59, the CSB includes a word that adds some helpful insight to our understanding. It says, "I...turned my steps *back* to your decrees" (emphasis mine). In considering his ways, he realizes that he is on the wrong path and quickly turns back to the Lord in repentance. God is quick to forgive, which means we can be quick to repent, confident that He will be compassionate and kind toward us in our weakness. No matter how often the wicked ensnare him and lead him astray, the psalmist is determined to keep returning to the law of the Lord. He practices praise so frequently that it becomes his first instinct, keeping his mind and heart fixed on the righteousness of God even when he wakes in the middle of the night. As part of his resolve to walk in obedience, the psalmist also seeks friendship with those who will exhort him in the ways of God, spurring him on in his faith. As a result, he sees the steadfast love of the Lord in every place and situation, filling the earth. Yet he ends this stanza by asking the Lord to teach him more because he knows he has only begun learning, only scratching the surface of the knowledge of the Most High God.

Application

- Would it be enough for you if you inherited nothing in this life but Christ? It is easy to know the right answer, yet we too often desire Jesus *along with* other things that compete for His place in our hearts. As you search your heart today, confess any disproportionate affections or desires revealed by the Holy Spirit.

- What kind of community have you surrounded yourself with? Do your friends draw you closer to Christ or pull you away from Him?

49

HETH | PRAYER

Heavenly Father,

I confess that my heart is not always, or even often, faithful to You as my greatest love. I do not value You as I ought, and therefore I do not worship You as I ought. Forgive my heart's wandering, and help me to love You more deeply and truly with each day.

Help me to be quick to turn back in repentance when I have sinned. I know that You love me steadfastly and that because of Jesus, You are faithful and just to forgive when I humbly confess my sin to You.

Thank You for Your Word. Continue to teach me more of Yourself day by day.

Amen.

The earth, O Lord,
is full of your
steadfast love;
teach me your statutes!

Psalm 119:64

Psalm 119:65-72

TETH

65 You have dealt well with your servant,

O Lord, according to your word.

66 Teach me good judgment and knowledge,

for I believe in your commandments.

67 Before I was afflicted I went astray,

but now I keep your word.

68 You are good and do good;

teach me your statutes.

69 The insolent smear me with lies,

but with my whole heart I keep your precepts;

70 their heart is unfeeling like fat,

but I delight in your law.

71 It is good for me that I was afflicted,

that I might learn your statutes.

72 The law of your mouth is better to me

than thousands of gold and silver pieces.

Psalm 119:65-72

NOTES

Day 11

Psalm 119:65-72

1. Which word appears four times in this section?

2. List the things that the psalmist calls "good" in these verses:

3. What does the psalmist ask of God twice in this stanza (v. 66a, 68b)?

4. What has happened to the psalmist, which he refers to twice in this section (v. 67a, 71a)?

5. To what does he compare the law of God (v. 72)?

Devotional

In an Old Testament class I once took, when talking about the importance of repeated words when studying the Bible, the professor made the comment that sometimes our English translations do us a disservice in this regard. He said that translators sometimes actually try to make the text *less* repetitive by using synonyms for what is the same word in the Hebrew text, thus making it much harder for us to track keywords and themes. Another reason for varied word usage is when English grammar calls for a different word in order to form a proper sentence. This stanza of Psalm 119 is a prime example of this, as the Hebrew word translated as "good" (*ṭôḇ*) appears two other times here that may go unnoticed if you're not reading in the original language.

The psalmist begins by praising the Lord for His goodness to him. He sees how God has dealt well (*ṭôḇ*) with him, always according to what He has said He would do (v. 65). The writer of this psalm even looks back on a time when he suffered affliction and sees the goodness (*ṭôḇ*) of God in affliction, saying, "Before I went through this, I was pridefully wandering from Your ways, but

54

now I walk the path of obedience" (my paraphrase of v. 67). Because God is good (*tôḇ*), He can only do what is good (*tôḇ*) (v. 68), and here the psalmist sees the true goodness of God in sovereignly allowing him to suffer. He circles back to his time of affliction, making sure there is no question about what he is saying: it was *good* (*tôḇ*) that he was afflicted (v. 71) because it taught him obedience. I think of what the writer of Hebrews tells us:

> "[God] disciplines us for our good, that we may share his holiness. For the moment all discipline seems painful rather than pleasant, but later it yields the peaceful fruit of righteousness to those who have been trained by it."
> (Hebrews 12:10b–11)

This passage in Hebrews begins by talking about how imperfect, earthly fathers discipline their children and are respected for it because they love and care for their children. How much more will a perfect heavenly Father discipline the children He loves, and always for their good? Our God is a *good* Father who doesn't give us only what feels good to us but trains us in the way of righteousness by sovereignly ordaining hardship into our lives. He continually leads us toward holiness because He is holy.

The psalmist also asks for good knowledge and discernment as he relies on God's commands (v. 66). This is actually a slightly different Hebrew word (*ṭûḇ*), though it is translated here as "good." It finds its root in *ṭôḇ* but has a more superlative meaning. The psalmist is not simply asking for *good* judgment and knowledge but the *best*, which he knows lies only with the Source of all judgment and knowledge. This will enable him to rightly discern what is good, rather than what he only *perceives* as good.

Verses 69-70 present an interesting contrast between the psalmist and the insolent or arrogant. The insolent are cold and unfeeling and have been slandering him. But the psalmist remains wholehearted toward the Word of God, delighting in His instruction and continually seeking to learn more of Him. We, too, should rejoice in and treasure the Word of God, with hearts tender and moldable to His instruction.

Application

- Take a moment to think about a specific period of suffering you've walked through. What was your relationship with God like before that time? After?

- How do you discern what is good in your life? Do you evaluate based on your own perception and feelings, or do you filter everything through the truth of the Scriptures?

TETH | PRAYER

Father in heaven,

I thank You for Your goodness. Looking back on my life, I can see how even the suffering I have endured has drawn me closer to You and has taught me obedience.

I pray that I would trust Your heart through each trial, knowing that You are a good and wise Father. Help me not to be hard-hearted or prideful but to trust You to do the good and necessary work to sanctify my heart.

I ask that You make my "love abound more and more, with knowledge and all discernment," so that I can hold fast to what is good and remain pure before You, "filled with the fruit of righteousness that comes through Jesus Christ," to Your praise and glory (see Philippians 1:9-11).

Amen.

56

Before I was afflicted
I went astray,
but now I keep
your word.
Psalm 119:67

Psalm 119:73-80

YODH

73 Your hands have made and fashioned me;

give me understanding that I may learn your

commandments.

74 Those who fear you shall see me and rejoice,

because I have hoped in your word.

75 I know, O Lord, that your rules are righteous,

and that in faithfulness you have afflicted me.

76 Let your steadfast love comfort me

according to your promise to your servant.

77 Let your mercy come to me, that I may live;

for your law is my delight.

78 Let the insolent be put to shame,

because they have wronged me with falsehood;

as for me, I will meditate on your precepts.

79 Let those who fear you turn to me,

that they may know your testimonies.

80 May my heart be blameless in your statutes,

that I may not be put to shame!

Psalm 119:73-80

NOTES

Day 12

Psalm 119:73-80

1. How is the psalmist's view of God as Creator connected to his request for understanding (v. 73)?

2. Why do those who fear the Lord rejoice when they see the psalmist (v. 74)?

3. Fill in the following blanks from verse 75:

"I know, O Lord, that your _____ are _____,
and that in _____ you have _____ me."
(Psalm 119:75, ESV)

4. List the requests made by the psalmist in verses 76-80:

5. What small phrase is repeated in verses 78 and 80?

Devotional

As a parent, I spend a lot of time thinking about the best way to help my children understand the things I'm trying to teach them—both biblical truth and practical life skills—and why it's important for them to learn obedience. Because each child is vastly different, each one responds better to different parenting methods, word phrasing, tone, and even different consequences for disobedience. Because God is our Creator, He doesn't have to spend time figuring out what works for each of us; He already knows us better than we even know ourselves. He knows how He created each of our minds to work, and therefore, He knows exactly what each of us needs and how best to open our minds and hearts to understand His instructions.

Sometimes, the Lord grants us understanding by sovereignly allowing us to walk through suffering. Think about those in your life whose faith you most admire and who cause you to rejoice at their hope in the Lord. Most often, this kind of deep and abiding faith is a direct result of having suffered some kind of affliction or grief. The psalmist recognizes this as he says, "Those who fear you shall see me and rejoice, because I have hoped in your word" (v. 74). It is a joy to get to witness the faith of others as they hope in the Lord, and especially so through affliction. When we are the ones suffering, we have the opportunity to put God's faithfulness on display as we set our hope in His steadfast love. Because He is righteous—free of sin and injustice—we can trust what He allows to be good for us. God is faithful when He protects or delivers us from affliction, and He remains faithful when He allows it (v. 75). Suffering is never pleasant or easy, but as we preach the truth of the Scriptures to ourselves, we are reminded that we can *trust* our faithful and good Creator.

As the psalmist reminds himself of God's character, he is comforted in his pain. God's mercy is his source of life, and God's steadfast love is a balm to his soul. Though he delights in the law of the Lord, he is also acutely aware of his inability to keep it. He humbly prays, "Let your mercy come to me, that I may live" (v. 77) because he knows that apart from God's mercy, we have no hope of life. As the psalmist learns to obey faithfully in all circumstances, he has no need to fear being put to shame like those who reject God's statutes (v. 78, 80; see also Psalm 25:3). He then circles back around to the desire to bolster others in their faith, praying that his steadfastness in affliction can be an encouragement to those around him who also fear the Lord. In asking that he not be put to shame, this writer is not seeking to exalt his own name but that of the One he lives for. Our psalmist's greatest desire is to lift high the name of the Lord through a life of faithfulness.

Application

- Paul tells us in 2 Corinthians that God "comforts us in all our affliction, so that we may be able to comfort those who are in any kind of affliction, through the comfort we ourselves receive from God" (2 Cor. 1:4). Have you had the opportunity to share your story with anyone? Be looking for an opportunity this week to share with someone about God's faithfulness to you.

- Which attribute or characteristic of the Lord brings you comfort today? Spend a few moments now praising Him for it.

61

YODH | PRAYER

Lord,

May my life encourage other believers in hardship as they see me remain steadfast in hope, trusting in You, my faithful God. I pray that You would make my life an example to others of the goodness of You and Your Word.

Thank You for Your great mercy, for without it, I would be utterly lost. Give me the grace needed to learn faithful obedience through whatever You ordain for each of my days. I love You, Lord.

Amen.

Those who fear you shall see me and *rejoice,* because I have hoped in your word.

Psalm 119:74

Psalm 119:81–88

KAPH

81 My soul longs for your salvation;

 I hope in your word.

82 My eyes long for your promise;

 I ask, "When will you comfort me?"

83 For I have become like a wineskin in the smoke,

 yet I have not forgotten your statutes.

84 How long must your servant endure?

 When will you judge those who persecute me?

85 The insolent have dug pitfalls for me;

 they do not live according to your law.

86 All your commandments are sure;

 they persecute me with falsehood; help me!

87 They have almost made an end of me on earth,

 but I have not forsaken your precepts.

88 In your steadfast love give me life,

 that I may keep the testimonies of your mouth.

Psalm 119:81-88

NOTES

Day 13

Psalm 119:81-88

1. For what two things does the psalmist say he longs (vv. 81-82)?

2. In response to his longings, what does he ask the Lord (v. 82b)?

3. What does the metaphor, "I have become like a wineskin in the smoke," mean (v. 83)?

4. What have the psalmist's enemies done to him (vv. 84-87)?

5. What has he held fast to in the face of persecution (v. 83b, 87b)?

Devotional

Yesterday we watched our psalmist remain steadfast through affliction. Here we see that, though he has not given up hope, he is feeling the weariness that continuous suffering brings. We see him appear to vacillate between despair and hope, weariness and faith. He longs for God's promised salvation as he begs God for comfort. Yet he holds onto his hope in God's Word. He says he has become "like a wineskin dried by smoke" (v. 83), feeling dried up, exhausted, and useless. Yet the Scriptures are not only intended to be a list of rules to obey; they are meant to give us hope and rest when we feel weary and burdened. This hope is not a wistful mindset of, "I hope this will happen," but "My hope is set on this because I *know* it is sure." The psalmist is not hoping that the Lord will deliver him but waiting expectantly to see it happen, actively looking for Him to work. The God of this psalmist is the same God that we worship today, and His promises will always stand firm because He is trustworthy.

66

Amidst his faith, the psalmist doesn't downplay his pain and exhaustion. He begs God to show up in judgment on those who are afflicting him. We can feel his frustration as he continues to face persecution, but he knows where his help comes from (see Psalm 121:1-2). He struggles to be patient with the Lord's timing as he sees the insolent continually rebelling against God's law. Though it appears that the wicked are about to win the day, the psalmist holds onto the Lord with everything he has. Even in his dried-up state of heart, mind, body, and soul, he clings to what he *knows* to be true: God is faithful. As he talks honestly with the Lord about his struggles, he gently guides his heart back to the truth that God's love is steadfast and His decrees are completely trustworthy.

Application

- In Matthew 11:28, Jesus says, "Come to me, all of you who are weary and burdened, and I will give you rest." Where do you turn when you feel weary? Do you run to Jesus, or do you seek comfort and rest in the things of this world?

- How do you pray when you're weary, frustrated, angry, or impatient? Is prayer just a place to vent your emotions? Or do you follow the pattern of the psalmists (not just this one!), rehearsing the truth to your heart while honestly talking with God about your struggles?

KAPH | PRAYER

Dear Jesus,

When I am weary and worn, help me to remember to run to You for rest. Help me to look to You as my help and to find strength and comfort in the truths of Your Word as I abide in Your presence.

I long for Your return, when You will defeat sin and death once and for all, making all things new. It can be hard to wait for that glorious day with patience, as wickedness so often seems to be winning. Yet I know that You are good and faithful, trustworthy and true. You will come at just the right time, and You will win, for You have already won.

Thank You for loving me steadfastly. Help me to live in faithful obedience to Your Word as I wait for You.

Amen.

In your steadfast love *give me life,* that I may keep the *testimonies* of your mouth.

Psalm 119:88

Psalm 119:89-96

LAMEDH

89 Forever, O Lord, your word

    is firmly fixed in the heavens.

90 Your faithfulness endures to all generations;

    you have established the earth, and it stands fast.

91 By your appointment they stand this day,

    for all things are your servants.

92 If your law had not been my delight,

    I would have perished in my affliction.

93 I will never forget your precepts,

    for by them you have given me life.

94 I am yours; save me,

    for I have sought your precepts.

95 The wicked lie in wait to destroy me,

    but I consider your testimonies.

96 I have seen a limit to all perfection,

    but your commandment is exceedingly broad.

Psalm 119:89-96

NOTES

Day 14

Psalm 119:89-96

1. Fill in the following blanks from verses 89-91:
   "Forever, O Lord, your word
   is _____ _____ in the heavens.
   Your faithfulness _____ to all generations;
   you have established the earth, and it _____ _____.
   By your appointment they _____ this day,
   for all things are your servants."
   (Psalm 119:89-91, ESV)

2. What does the psalmist say would have happened had he not delighted in God's law (v. 92)?

3. Why does he say he will never forget the Lord's precepts (v. 93)?

4. What does he consider when threatened by the wicked (v. 95)?

5. In verse 96, what does the psalmist mean by the statement, "I have seen a limit to all perfection"?

Devotional

In verses 89-91, we see several synonyms used to describe the Lord and the absolute security of everything He does and says. The psalmist speaks of the vastness of the universe and how it all displays the great faithfulness of God. He looks back over the course of history and sees the enduring faithfulness of the Lord to His people. Creation continues its work in faithfulness because of its faithful Creator. His judgments stand firm because the faithful God is the One who spoke them. From all of these truths, we can see that God is the only One whose works will last. Our security must not be found in the temporary

72

things of this world, which will pass away when their time is through, but in the One who is eternal and whose faithfulness endures for all of time and beyond (see Psalm 117:2; Matthew 24:35).

Several times previously, the psalmist has asked God to give him life (see v. 25, 37, 40, 88). In verses 92-93, he recognizes that he *has been given* life through God's precepts. He credits his delight in God's law with sustaining him through affliction and suffering. He knows the abundance of living by faith, has tasted and seen the goodness of God, and vows never to forget the teaching of the Scriptures as he sees the vast benefit he has gained from them.

Our psalmist then makes a bold request. He knows that God has promised to save His people (see v. 41; also Deuteronomy 7:12). He asks for salvation based on his continued faithfulness to seek the Lord in every circumstance. He knows that the wicked will not ultimately prosper because the Lord has promised to save and bless His own, though His timetable doesn't always match ours.

The psalmist ends this stanza by circling back to the eternality of God. Even the most perfect things on this earth are finite and limited. There is only One who has no limit. As imperfect humans who give imperfect rules, it is hard for us to comprehend rules with no loopholes or exceptions, and some commands can be hard to understand. This is where we must come to know and trust the character of the One who has given us the commands found in His Word, knowing that He is a good, faithful, and wise Father who instructs us for our true benefit. Our God is good and faithful beyond all measure and so, too, are His instructions.

Application

- Where is your security found? In this ever-changing world, the only true source of security is the One who is the same yesterday, today, and forever (see Hebrews 13:8). Take some time to search your heart and confess any misplaced trust, fully surrendering your life and future to God's wise and good hands.

- Which of the Lord's commands is hard for you to believe is good, and why? Spend some time today meditating on the goodness of the One who gave that command, allowing the Holy Spirit to soften your heart to His good instruction.

73

LAMEDH | PRAYER

Dear Lord,

Thank You that Your Word is trustworthy because it will never pass away and that You are trustworthy because You never change.

Please forgive me for all the times I trust in anything other than You. Help me to find my security in You alone. My life and my future are in Your hands, Lord. I know that You are faithful and good, and I trust Your sovereignty.

Amen.

74

Forever, O Lord, your word is firmly fixed in the heavens.
Psalm 119:89

Psalm 119:97-104

MEM

97 Oh how I love your law!

It is my meditation all the day.

98 Your commandment makes me wiser than my

enemies,

for it is ever with me.

99 I have more understanding than all my teachers,

for your testimonies are my meditation.

100 I understand more than the aged,

for I keep your precepts.

101 I hold back my feet from every evil way,

in order to keep your word.

102 I do not turn aside from your rules,

for you have taught me.

103 How sweet are your words to my taste,

sweeter than honey to my mouth!

104 Through your precepts I get understanding;

therefore I hate every false way.

Psalm 119:97-104

NOTES

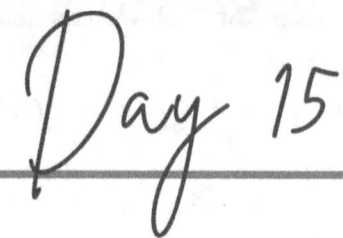

Day 15

Psalm 119:97–104

1. How often does the psalmist meditate on the law of God, and what does this tell us about his heart (v. 97)?

2. Who are the groups of people that the psalmist claims to have more understanding and wisdom than (vv. 98-100)?

3. Finish the following phrases from verses 101-102:
   - I _____ from every evil way (v. 101)
   - I _____ from your rules (v. 102)

4. Why does the psalmist do these things (vv. 101-103)?

5. Through what does the psalmist gain understanding (v. 104)?

Devotional

When Moses taught the Law to the Israelites, he told them that their adherence to God's statutes would make them wise in the sight of all people (see Deuteronomy 4:5-8). In Psalm 119, the psalmist sees the truth of this in his own life hundreds of years later. As he continually abides with God through meditation on and obedience to His Word, he is not only made wiser than his enemies but even his teachers and elders. Godly wisdom does not simply come with age but through the opening of our eyes to behold wondrous things from the Scriptures (see Psalm 119:18). The psalmist keeps God's instruction with him (v. 98), meditates on it (v. 99), and ultimately obeys it (v. 100). This is the essence of true wisdom.

In this section, we also see the cycle of time spent in the Word of God and the effect it has on our lives. The fact that the psalmist is holding back his feet from evil and refraining from turning aside from righteousness implies that he faces the temptation to do otherwise. But because of his love for God's law, he is able to stay on the path of obedience. Faithful obedience over time turns into *delighted* obedience. As we rightly value the Lord, we will value what He has said. As we learn to love Him with all our heart, we will, in turn, love His words to us, and we will be able to say with the psalmist, "How sweet are your words to my taste, sweeter than honey to my mouth!" (v. 103). Consistent time spent dwelling on the Scriptures becomes obedience as the power of God's Word transforms our hearts. Obedience becomes a delight as we recognize the true goodness and wisdom of the Scriptures, and this delight brings us back again and again as we taste the sweetness of the Lord's words.

There is a great contrast encompassing this stanza. The psalmist begins by saying that he *loves* God's instruction (v. 97) and ends by saying that he *hates* every false way (v. 104). When we allow the Word of God to change our hearts, we will begin to find that the ways of the world and the enemy have become detestable to us in comparison with the sweetness of the Lord and His goodness. As the Holy Spirit warms our cold and calloused hearts to the things of Christ, we will continually become more like Him, learning to love what He loves and hate what He hates.

Application

- Wisdom is described here as loving and obeying the Scriptures. Based on this definition, are you walking in wisdom, or are there areas of your life in which you're going your own way?

- Romans 12:1-2 instructs us to present ourselves as a living sacrifice, holy and acceptable before God, letting Him transform our hearts by renewing our minds so that we can discern what is good and acceptable. How soft (or hard) is your heart, friend? Do you love what God loves and hate what He hates? Do you call good what God has called good and evil what He has called evil?

MEM | PRAYER

Lord,

Help me to be consistent in spending time learning from Your Word, but not just to gain more knowledge. Let the wisdom of the Scriptures change me as I learn to love You more.

Keep my heart soft to Your instruction through Your Holy Spirit. Make Your words sweeter to my taste than the things of this world, and help me to walk in faithful obedience.

Amen.

How *sweet* are your
words to my taste,
sweeter than *honey*
to my mouth!
Psalm 119:103

Psalm 119:105–112

NUN

105 Your word is a lamp to my feet

and a light to my path.

106 I have sworn an oath and confirmed it,

to keep your righteous rules.

107 I am severely afflicted;

give me life, O Lord, according to your word!

108 Accept my freewill offerings of praise, O Lord,

and teach me your rules.

109 I hold my life in my hand continually,

but I do not forget your law.

110 The wicked have laid a snare for me,

but I do not stray from your precepts.

111 Your testimonies are my heritage forever,

for they are the joy of my heart.

112 I incline my heart to perform your statutes

forever, to the end.

Psalm 119:105-112

NOTES

Day 16

Psalm 119:105-112

1. What does the psalmist call God's Word in verse 105?

2. What has he sworn to do (v. 106)?

3. What does the psalmist ask of the Lord in verse 108?

4. What danger(s) does the psalmist face (vv. 109-110)?

5. Fill in the following blanks from verse 111:
   "Your testimonies are my _____ forever,
   for they are the _____ of my _____."
   (Psalm 119:111, ESV)

Devotional

The verses we're studying today hold a strong undertone of deliberate commitment to God and His Word. We have discussed this in previous stanzas, but it bears repeating: devotion to the Lord never happens by accident. A faithful life will only happen on purpose.

In the previous stanza, the psalmist describes himself as walking the straight and narrow, not turning from God's judgments or straying to evil paths. He begins this stanza by showing us how this is possible: he lets the Scriptures light his way. They are a lamp to our feet that guides us into all truth (v. 105), and when we acknowledge the wisdom of the Lord in all our ways, He truly directs our paths and makes them straight (see Proverbs 3:5-6). Even in severe affliction, the psalmist is resolved to keep the law of God. This is not because of his own goodness, but simply because he sees the rightness of God's law. He knows that because the Lord is righteous, His rules must be as well.

After considering his resolve to keep the law, he asks the Lord to accept his freewill offerings of praise (v. 108). Rather than a sacrifice required by the

84

Mosaic law, the mark of the freewill offering was the giver's stirred heart and willing spirit.[8] Our psalmist longs for his praise to be acceptable before the God he loves. He is not focused on himself, how he feels, or what he enjoys, but on the One he is praising. He wants nothing but to please his Lord and bring glory to His great name, and only that which is given from this heart posture can truly be called praise.

Verses 109-110 speak of the inherent danger the psalmist continually finds himself in. Amid danger, attack, and entrapment, he holds fast to the Word of God as his strength and stability. The psalmist ends this section by speaking of the Scriptures as meeting his greatest desire. His truest and deepest joy is found in the Lord. He feels no need for any inheritance other than the very words of his God. Knowing and meditating on God's Word brings him such utter delight that he is satisfied for this to be his only heritage. The psalmist views the right relationship with God, resulting from obedience to His commands, as the only reward, riches, or inheritance needed for all eternity.

Application

- What is your praise like? Do you consider whether it is acceptable to the Lord, or do you only consider whether or not you find it enjoyable?

- Is God enough for you? It is so easy to say, "Yes!" while still living as though we need God and _____ (fill in the blank). Ask the Lord to search your heart today and reveal any desires or "rewards" you are holding up alongside Him. Confess those things before Him and ask Him to help you learn to be truly satisfied in Him alone.

---

8. *Holman Illustrated Bible Dictionary, Revised and Expanded*, ed. Chad Brand et al., s.v. "freewill offering," (Nashville, TN: B&H Publishing Group, 2015), page 594.

NUN | PRAYER

Heavenly Father,

Guide me by Your Word. Let the Scriptures be a light for my path, keeping me walking in the way of righteousness.

Make my praise acceptable in Your sight, bringing glory and honor to Your great and holy name. Help me to want nothing more than to be in a right relationship with You. Satisfy my heart with Your unfailing love.

Amen.

Your testimonies are
my heritage forever,
for they are the
joy of my heart.

Psalm 119:111

Day 17

Psalm 119

1. Take a few minutes to read through the entire psalm.

2. Optional notations to make as you read:
   - *Requests made to God*
   - *References to time (before dawn, at all times, to the end, forever, etc.)*

3. Take note of any repeated words or phrases.

The Lord my portion.

PS. 119:57

89

Psalm 119:113-120

SAMEKH

113 I hate the double-minded,

but I love your law.

114 You are my hiding place and my shield;

I hope in your word.

115 Depart from me, you evildoers,

that I may keep the commandments of my God.

116 Uphold me according to your promise,

that I may live,

and let me not be put to shame in my hope!

117 Hold me up, that I may be safe

and have regard for your statutes continually!

118 You spurn all who go astray from your statutes,

for their cunning is in vain.

119 All the wicked of the earth you discard like dross,

therefore I love your testimonies.

120 My flesh trembles for fear of you,

and I am afraid of your judgments.

Psalm 119:113-120

NOTES

Day 18

Psalm 119:113-120

1. In verse 113, who does the psalmist say he hates, and in contrast, what does he love? Is this a fair contrast? Why or why not?

2. What does he call the Lord in verse 114?

3. What does he ask God to do in this stanza?

4. What does the psalmist say the Lord does to the wicked who stray from His commands (vv. 118-119)?

5. What two synonyms are found in verse 120, and what are they used in reference to?

Devotional

Our selection today begins with the psalmist saying that he hates those who are double-minded. This may seem harsh, but the New Testament helps us a little as we dig into what this means. The double-minded are filled with doubt and therefore unable to please God since without faith, it is impossible to please Him (see Js. 1:5-8, Heb. 11:6). One lexicon defines the double-minded as those who are "destitute of firm faith."[9] They are unstable, having divided loyalty in their mind, with no secure truth to abide by. God's law is not so. It not only contains truth; it *is* truth, steady and unchanging because of the One who gave it. The double-minded have no love for the law because they have no love for its Giver. Where their faith is found lacking, the faith of those who love God and His commands grows ever stronger.

9. *Gesenius' Hebrew-Chaldee Lexicon*, as quoted under "H5588 - sē'ēp̄ - Strong's Hebrew Lexicon (esv)." Blue Letter Bible. Accessed 3 Jul, 2024. https://www.blueletterbible.org/lexicon/h5588/esv/wlc/0-1/

We are again seeing the heart of our psalmist drawn toward what God loves, and away from what displeases Him. He runs to God for shelter, setting his hope in God's Word and avoiding those who oppose the truth. Of this, C.H. Spurgeon says, "Those who make a conscience of their thoughts are not likely to tolerate evil company."[10] This is not referring to those who might be ignorant and need to hear the gospel (though we should likewise use wisdom and discretion as we interact with those individuals). This is speaking specifically of those who might influence our lives while living in direct opposition to the truth, running far from the Lord as they pursue their own evil desires. The psalmist's motive for this decision is important, which we find in the second half of verse 115. The wicked were hindering his ability to obey the Lord, and this is what determined his choice of company. Anyone or anything that kept him from wholeheartedly keeping God's commands needed to be removed from his life. Interestingly, this is the only place in this entire psalm where the personal word "my" is used alongside the name of God, which is significant. To quote Spurgeon again:

> "Because Jehovah is our God therefore we resolve to obey him, and to chase out of our sight those who would hinder us in his service...God's law is our pleasure when the God of the law is our God."[11]

As the psalmist forms his prayers, he relies heavily on both the promises and character of his God. We know that these prayers will have been answered favorably because God cannot act in any way that contradicts who He is or what He has said. Our beloved psalmist will not be "put to shame in [his] hope" (v. 116) because his hope is in the right place!

> "Indeed, none who wait for you shall be put to shame; they shall be ashamed who are wantonly treacherous."
> (Psalm 25:3)

This psalmist knows that, in the end, all the deceit of the wicked is empty and worthless. If they are opposing the Word of God—having gone "astray from [God's] statutes" (v. 118)—they cannot be in a right relationship with God Himself, and this leads to dire consequences. Ultimately they will face the judgment of the Lord, discarded like scum (see v. 119). In contrast, the psalmist holds a healthy fear of the Lord and of His Word. He knows that "it is a terrifying thing to fall into the hands of the living God" (Hebrews 10:31). If we truly fear the Lord, we will also have an appropriate fear and respect for what He has said.

---

10. Spurgeon, C. "Psalm 119 Verses 113-120 by C. H. Spurgeon." Blue Letter Bible. Last Modified 5 Dec 2016. https://www.blueletterbible.org/Comm/spurgeon_charles/tod/ps119_113-120.cfm
11. Ibid.

Application

- How is your relationship with the Scriptures? Though it is obviously not the only test, this can be a helpful gauge of whether your heart is right with the Lord. Do you regularly spend time with Him through His Word?

- How is the company you keep? Who do you allow to influence your life? Do they walk in faithfulness and encourage you to do the same, or do they tempt you toward sin as they disregard God's commands?

SAMEKH | PRAYER

Father in Heaven,

I pray that You would help me to please
You with a heart full of faith, my hope
set firmly in Your Word. I pray that I
would not be double-minded and
unstable but steady: certain of who You
are and of the infallible truth of the
Scriptures.

Help me to humbly and wholeheartedly
obey You, embracing what You have said
is good and right, even when it feels
difficult, inconvenient, or unpopular.
Give me the courage and strength to cut
out anything that pulls my heart
toward sin. Help me to fear You more
than I fear those around me.

Amen.

Psalm 119:121-128

AYIN

121 I have done what is just and right;

do not leave me to my oppressors.

122 Give your servant a pledge of good;

let not the insolent oppress me.

123 My eyes long for your salvation

and for the fulfillment of your righteous promise.

124 Deal with your servant according to your

steadfast love,

and teach me your statutes.

125 I am your servant; give me understanding,

that I may know your testimonies!

126 It is time for the Lord to act,

for your law has been broken.

127 Therefore I love your commandments

above gold, above fine gold.

128 Therefore I consider all your precepts to be right;

I hate every false way.

Psalm 119:121-128

NOTES

Day 19

Psalm 119:121-128

1. What requests does the psalmist make of God in this stanza?

2. Is the psalmist being presumptuous when he requests a pledge of good (ESV) or a guarantee of his well-being (CSB) from the Lord (v. 122)? Why or why not?

3. What promise is he referring to in verse 123?

4. What is the psalmist angry about in verse 126?

5. What two "therefore" statements are made in verses 127-128 (ESV)?
- *Therefore* _____
- *Therefore* _____

Devotional

The psalmist boldly asks the Lord to act according to His justice in today's section. He doesn't want vengeance for himself but justice according to the law for the honor of the Lord's name. Our psalmist is fed up with a world overrun by evil and is ready for Divine action to be taken. In this way, he experiences a personal revival as he is stirred up with intensified love for God and His righteous commands. One outworking of this is hatred of all that is contrary to God's holiness. If we truly love the Lord and His precepts, which are our standard for truth and right living, then we will oppose everything that contradicts the truth of the Scriptures.

After asking for justice, the psalmist asks the Lord to give him "a pledge of good" (v. 122). The phrase in Hebrew translates as, "Be surety for your servant

98

for good."[12] Though this phrasing feels a little awkward in English, I think it greatly helps our understanding of this verse. The Lord has promised good to His children. This is not to say that He has promised everything will look the way that we think is good, but that because He has promised *Himself* to us, we know that we already have all that is good. We have no good apart from Him, but because He is good, in Him we have all we'll ever need. The Lord withholds no good thing from us (see Ps. 84:11) because He has already given us Himself. He is the guarantee of our good because He *is* our good.

Next, the psalmist says his eyes long for the Lord's promised salvation and asks Him to show His steadfast love by teaching him the statutes of the Scriptures. He knows that God is faithful to do what He has promised, so he keeps his eyes open, watching for the promised Messiah. He sees gaining a greater understanding of God's Word as an outworking of God's faithful love. The Lord has not given us His instruction as a burden but as a gift of kindness out of His steadfast love for us! While He does ask us to surrender our wills to His, our gracious heavenly Father doesn't require blind obedience from us. He has given us His Word, which is so much more than just a list of rules. He has recorded a history of Himself as He relates to His people so that we can not only obey Him but *know* Him and, therefore, know the true goodness and wisdom of His commands.

Suddenly, the psalmist shows his zeal for the law of the Lord and asks Him to come in judgment on those who are breaking it. He is not angry at his own affliction or hurt but at the blatant disregard for God and His Word. Because he deeply loves the Lord and recognizes the magnitude of His wrath toward sin, our psalmist deeply reveres God's commandments, valuing them more highly even than the finest gold. Consequently, he sees the rightness of the Scriptures and hates "every false way" (v. 128). Once our eyes are opened to the truth, we become averse to anything that opposes it.

Application

- **What is your standard for truth and right living? This question is crucial in today's world, in which it is so prevalent to "call evil good and good evil" (Is. 5:20). Be sure that you daily fasten on the belt of truth so that you are "able to withstand in the evil day," (see Eph. 6:10-14).**

- **As the psalmist's eyes longed to see the Messiah come and save His people, so our eyes should long to see our Savior come back and make all things new, crying out, "Come quickly, Lord Jesus!" Are your eyes open, expectantly watching for Christ's promised return?**

---

12. *NET Bible, Full Notes Edition* (Nashville, TN: Thomas Nelson, 2019), page 1044.

AYIN | PRAYER

Gracious Father,

May Your Word be my standard as I seek to live by Your truth. As I hold fast to Your commands, let my life be a light that points others to You in this dark world.

I pray that Christ will soon return to rid the world of brokenness and sin. In the meantime, help me trust that You are with me and that Your presence is enough for me—the only good I need.

Amen.

My eyes long for your

salvation

and for the fulfillment of your righteous promise.
Psalm 119:123

Psalm 119:129–136

PE

129 Your testimonies are wonderful;

therefore my soul keeps them.

130 The unfolding of your words gives light;

it imparts understanding to the simple.

131 I open my mouth and pant,

because I long for your commandments.

132 Turn to me and be gracious to me,

as is your way with those who love your name.

133 Keep steady my steps according to your promise,

and let no iniquity get dominion over me.

134 Redeem me from man's oppression,

that I may keep your precepts.

135 Make your face shine upon your servant,

and teach me your statutes.

136 My eyes shed streams of tears,

because people do not keep your law.

Psalm 119:129-136

NOTES

Day 20

Psalm 119:129-136

1. Why does the psalmist keep God's instructions (v. 129)?

2. Verse 130 mentions two things given by the words of God. What are they?

3. According to the psalmist, what is God's practice with those who love His name (v. 132)?

4. In verse 133, what two things does the psalmist ask the Lord to do?

5. What other requests are made in verses 134-135?

Devotional

I love how this section begins; it sets the stage for the unfolding of this stanza along with the next. The Lord has answered our psalmist's earlier prayer, having opened his eyes to behold wondrous things from His law (see v. 18). Because he knows that God's decrees are good and wonderful, he wholeheartedly obeys them. He has experienced the impact of the Scriptures on his life, seeing how they provide wisdom and light his path, and he longs for more of this. He has tasted and seen that the Lord is good, and he can't get enough. He longs for the goodness of the Lord to completely saturate his life.

A string of requests is made to God in verses 132-135. The first is simply for the Lord to turn to him and be gracious to him. God has revealed Himself in the past as One who is gracious to those who love His name (see Exodus 34:6), and the psalmist calls upon this truth. He knows that the Lord is gracious and is simply asking Him to act out of that nature. Next, he asks God to steady his steps, not letting any sin get dominion over him. He knows that "no one can serve two masters" (Matt. 6:24), and "you are slaves of the one whom you obey, either of sin, which leads to death, or of obedience, which leads to righteousness" (Rom. 6:16). He's asking the Lord to deliver him from slavery to sin *so that* he is free to walk in obedience. On this side of the Cross, we get to see the answer to this prayer, as sin no longer has dominion over us in Christ! When we are in Christ, it is not our effort but the Holy Spirit that keeps our steps steady on the path of obedience. It is God's faithfulness to us that enables our faithfulness to Him.

The psalmist keeps his eyes and heart set on the Lord. When he says, "Make your face shine upon your servant" (v. 135), he is asking for the Lord's favor and blessing, specifically in the form of teaching. He loves the Lord and understands that loving God means obeying His commands, made easier by gaining a deeper understanding of them. He is truly heartbroken to see people living in opposition to God's law, knowing that "their end is destruction...with minds set on earthly things" (Phil. 3:19).

Application

- If you are in Christ, He has freed you from sin. It no longer holds any power over you, for you are a new creation; you are free to obey! Are there any areas where your old nature has pulled you away from the path of obedience? Repent, and ask the Holy Spirit for help to walk in faithfulness today.

- Where is your focus? Is your mind set on things above or earthly things (see Colossians 3:1-3)?

PE | PRAYER

Dear Lord,

Thank You for the instruction You have given through the Scriptures and for opening my eyes to behold wondrous things in it. Apart from You, I am foolish, lacking understanding and wisdom. Enlighten the eyes of my heart (see Ephesians 1:18) with the truth of Your Word.

I confess the ways that I have allowed my feet to wander from your commands, and I ask You to forgive me. Thank You for Your faithfulness, even when I am unfaithful. Strengthen me through Your grace to walk in faithful obedience today.

Amen.

Turn to me and be
gracious
to me, as is your way
with those who love
your name.
Psalm 119:132

Psalm 119:137–144

TSADHE

137 Righteous are you, O Lord,

and right are your rules.

138 You have appointed your testimonies in

righteousness

and in all faithfulness.

139 My zeal consumes me,

because my foes forget your words.

140 Your promise is well tried,

and your servant loves it.

141 I am small and despised,

yet I do not forget your precepts.

142 Your righteousness is righteous forever,

and your law is true.

143 Trouble and anguish have found me out,

but your commandments are my delight.

144 Your testimonies are righteous forever;

give me understanding that I may live.

Psalm 119:137-144

NOTES

Day 21

Psalm 119:137-144

1. What word is used in various forms six times in this section?

2. What is the significance of the Lord's testimonies having been appointed in both righteousness *and* faithfulness (v. 138)?

3. How would you define "zeal," and what is causing this emotion in the psalmist (v. 139)?

4. What does it mean for something to be "well tried" (v. 140)?

5. What word comes after "righteous" in verses 142 and 144? Why does this matter?

Devotional

Today's stanza emphasizes righteousness, repeating various forms of the word five or six times in these eight verses, depending on which version you read. While the whole of Psalm 119 is centered on the Word of God, here, the psalmist turns our eyes toward the righteousness of God Himself, giving this as the foundation for our complete confidence in the rightness of God's instructions. If the Scriptures are the way God has chosen to reveal and express Himself, then it follows that His Word reflects His character. Verse 138 says, "You have appointed your testimonies in righteousness and in all faithfulness." The Hebrew word translated as "faithfulness" in this verse is closely related to the word translated as "true" in verse 142. Both words convey stability, certainty, trustworthiness, and faithfulness. The Lord has chosen to express and reveal Himself through the Scriptures. Therefore, as He is righteous, so also is His Word. As He is faithful, so also is His Word. It

110

would be contrary to God's very nature to give anything other than righteous commands. This means that because of His perfect righteousness, we can wholeheartedly trust His commands to be right and good. Everything this righteous God does is done in righteousness and can be trusted because of His faithfulness. He is both righteous *and* faithful, and in this, we find our security. The Lord will remain faithful to do what is right, and He will remain faithful to *us* as His beloved children.

In the very next breath, the psalmist expresses intense passion because his enemies disregard God's words: His instructions, commands, and laws. The Hebrew word translated as "zeal" is *qin'â*, which is most often used to refer to the jealousy of a spouse.[13] This is the good and right jealousy that comes as a result of a covenant relationship being violated. In the face of his enemies, the psalmist's first concern is not for himself but for the honor of the word of God.

He goes on to speak of the absolute purity of the Scriptures. When he says God's promise is well-tried, he is referring to the process of refining metal. As a goldsmith purges the impurities from gold or silver, so the Lord has ensured that His Word contains no imperfections. The Lord has shown Himself trustworthy again and again. Trusting Him is never an uncertainty, for His promise is well-tried, and His words have proven true. He will always pass the test of faithfulness.

Because he is fully convinced of the purity of God's Word, the psalmist declares that despite others' opinions of him, he will not forsake God's commands. Those who are faithful to hold the Scriptures in high regard are highly regarded by the Lord, however disliked or overlooked they may be by others.

The psalmist then returns to the righteousness of God and His law, expanding our understanding as he builds on what he has previously said. The Lord is not simply righteous but is righteous *forever*; His righteousness is eternally unchanging. The testimonies of the Lord are faithful and true, just as the God who gave them. Regardless of trouble and distress (v. 143), he finds comfort and joy as he delights in the steady and unchanging words of his God. Because of this, his prayer is not for deliverance from trouble as much as it is for a greater understanding of the law of the Lord. He recognizes that true life is the everlasting life found through the very Word of God, which in the New Testament refers to Christ Himself: the only Way, Truth, and Life.[14] His greatest earthly longing is a deeper understanding of these righteous truths.

13. "H7068 - qin'â - Strong's Hebrew Lexicon (esv)." Blue Letter Bible. Accessed 13 Jul, 2024. https://www.blueletterbible.org/lexicon/h7068/esv/wlc/0-1/
14. See John 1:1-4; 14:6.

Application

- Do you truly believe all of God's commands to be good, given in righteousness? It is easy to say "yes," yet so often, we live in a way that is contradictory to this, revealing our true beliefs. Spend some time in conversation with the Lord today, searching your heart for ways that you live as though you know better than your Creator. Humbly confess those things before Him, knowing that He and His Word are good and altogether trustworthy.

- Suffering can cause us to go one of two ways: rejecting our faith because it didn't work or clinging to it more tightly because it is all we have left. Do you turn away from God's Word or find greater delight in it when you face hardship?

TSADHE | PRAYER

Dear Lord,

Help me to live from the belief that Your commands are trustworthy simply because they are from You—a holy God and a good Father who loves His children. You have proven Yourself faithful time and time again, and I know that You will remain faithful forever.

Give me a greater understanding of the Scriptures and a greater delight in You as I see more of who You are through Your Word.

Amen.

Psalm 119:145-152

QOPH

145 With my whole heart I cry; answer me, O Lord!

    I will keep your statutes.

146 I call to you; save me,

    that I may observe your testimonies.

147 I rise before dawn and cry for help;

    I hope in your words.

148 My eyes are awake before the watches of the night,

    that I may meditate on your promise.

149 Hear my voice according to your steadfast love;

    O Lord, according to your justice give me life.

150 They draw near who persecute me with evil

    purpose;

    they are far from your law.

151 But you are near, O Lord,

    and all your commandments are true.

152 Long have I known from your testimonies

    that you have founded them forever.

Psalm 119:145-152

NOTES

Day 22

Psalm 119:145-152

1. What attitude does the psalmist display in verses 145-146?

2. What times of day are referenced in verses 147-148? What does this convey to you about the psalmist's habits?

3. What two characteristics of the Lord are specifically mentioned (v. 149)?

4. What contrasting words or ideas do you notice (vv. 150-151)?

5. Fill in the blanks from verse 151 below:
   "But you are _____, O Lord,
   and _____ your commandments are _____."
   (Psalm 119:151, ESV)

Devotional

Early on in this psalm (see v. 2, 10), we saw the psalmist wholeheartedly seeking the Lord, and we see it again here as he cries out to the Lord for salvation. There is desperation in his tone; he is begging the Lord to pay attention and to act on his behalf. He is not just crying out for freedom's sake; the psalmist wants to have the freedom to *obey*. His relationship with the Lord is evident in this stanza as well. We see prayer's significant role alongside his devotion to the Scriptures and how each of these two aspects complements the other. Day and night, night and day, the psalmist is in continual communion with the Lord through prayer and the study of His Word. Both aspects are vital to a flourishing, abiding relationship with Yahweh. Without God's Word, we cannot know what we ought to expect or ask of God. Yet without prayer, the study of His Word is merely the pursuit of intellectual knowledge. Jen Wilkin puts it this way:

"Without prayer, our study is nothing but an intellectual pursuit. With prayer, it is a means of communing with the Lord. Prayer is what changes our study from the pursuit of knowledge to the pursuit of God Himself."[15]

As has been his pattern, the psalmist's prayer aligns with God's character. The Lord is just, and He abounds in steadfast love; it is these attributes that our psalmist appeals to as he prays (v. 149). This verse reminds us that our ability to pray does not rest on anything in us or that we have done but on God's steadfast love and faithfulness. What a comfort to know that He hears our prayers not because of our character but because of His!

There is a wonderful contrast in verses 150-151. The psalmist sees the wicked *drawing near* to inflict harm on him. In doing so, they run far from God's law (and, by extension, far from God Himself). Yet at the same time, the psalmist knows the Lord is *near* to all who call on Him in truth,[16] and His Word forever stands firm, regardless of the wickedness and deceit of humans (v. 152). In his distress, the psalmist recognizes the nearness of God even more plainly than that of his persecutors. He has experienced the faithfulness of the Lord through the truth of His Word, and this is his comfort in affliction. Though we may not be under direct attack by the wicked, this truth is for us today: God opposes the proud but gives grace to the humble. We can be sure that as we draw near to Him, He will faithfully draw near to us.[17]

Application

- How is your balance of prayer and study? If all of your time is spent in prayer, neglecting God's Word, you will know little of His character, and your theology will be sorely lacking. If you neglect to pray, all of that theological knowledge will be just that: head knowledge. We must be investing time in both prayer and study of the Scriptures if we are truly to grow in our relationship with God.

- Are you running in pride or drawing near in humility today? Are you holding parts of your life away from the Lord or humbly submitting everything to His will?

---

15. Jen Wilkin, *Women of the Word* (Wheaton, IL: Crossway, 2014), page 103.
16. See Psalm 145:18.
17. See James 4:6-8.

117

QOPH | PRAYER

Heavenly Father,

Help me to truly seek You as I study Your Word, rather than simply gaining more knowledge. Thank You for Your steadfast love and faithfulness which allow me to come before You in prayer.

Thank You for Your perfect justice, which means that because Jesus paid it all on the cross, You are faithful to forgive when I confess my sins to You.

I pray that I would know You are near and that I would lean on Your strength in every moment. I praise You because You are greater than my every care, anxiety, and need.

Amen.

I rise before dawn
and cry for help;
I *hope* in your words.
Psalm 119:147

119

Psalm 119:153-160

RESH

153 Look on my affliction and deliver me,

for I do not forget your law.

154 Plead my cause and redeem me;

give me life according to your promise!

155 Salvation is far from the wicked,

for they do not seek your statutes.

156 Great is your mercy, O Lord;

give me life according to your rules.

157 Many are my persecutors and my adversaries,

but I do not swerve from your testimonies.

158 I look at the faithless with disgust,

because they do not keep your commands.

159 Consider how I love your precepts!

Give me life according to your steadfast love.

160 The sum of your word is truth,

and every one of your righteous rules endures

forever.

Psalm 119:153-160

NOTES

Day 23

Psalm 119:153-160

1. What phrase is repeated three times in this section? Fill in the blanks below with the appropriate endings of each (all taken from the ESV):

"_____ ____ _____ *according to your* _____!" (v. 154)

"_____ ____ _____ *according to your* _____." (v. 156)

"_____ ____ _____ *according to your* _____ _____." (v. 159)

2. What does the psalmist say about the wicked in verse 155?

3. How does he describe God's mercy (v. 156)?

4. How does the psalmist feel about his faithless enemies, and why (vv. 157-158)?

5. Rewrite verse 160 in your own words.

Devotional

The psalmist again begins pleading with the Lord to rescue him from affliction, but his bigger request, repeated three times in this stanza, is for the Lord to give him life. At its core, this prayer woven throughout the entire psalm demonstrates the psalmist's deep sense of weakness and tendency to grow cold toward the Lord. He desperately needs the Lord in every moment of every day. He recognizes that it is not his own effort but rather the Lord who continually revives his heart with fresh affection and conviction.

After asking God to defend him, he turns his attention to those who are afflicting him, saying that salvation is far from them. The NET Bible translates this phrase even more directly, saying, "The wicked have no chance for deliverance." Of course, anyone can receive salvation by faith at any time, and none of us can achieve salvation through obedience because none of us is able to obey perfectly. But there is truth behind the idea that salvation is far from the wicked because they are actively opposing and running away from God.

Yet even as the psalmist considers these things, in the same breath, he remembers the great mercy of God. This matters deeply. We cannot rightly consider the fate of the wicked without recognizing how great the Lord's mercy has been toward *us*, for we, too, were once alienated from Christ, having no hope. We, too, were once far off but are now brought near by the blood of Jesus![18] Seeing that the wicked have little chance of being saved should not cause us to puff up in pride. Instead, we should fall to our knees in humble gratitude and awe at the God who is rich in mercy toward us. We who were once His enemies are now adopted as His beloved children through Christ.

The psalmist goes on to say that he is disgusted by the faithless. Faithlessness is a quality that reveals itself through a lack of obedience to God's Word. Disobedience is rooted in unbelief: doubting the character of God Himself. If we believed God to be good, we would trust Him to give good commands. If we believed that His commands are good, given by a loving Father for *our* good, we would wholeheartedly obey. Therefore, when we disobey, it is ultimately because we have not believed God to be who He says He is.

This stanza ends with a reminder of *why* God's Word is worthy of obedience:

> "The sum of your word is truth,
> and every one of your righteous rules endures forever."
> (Psalm 119:160)

The sum of God's Word—the entirety, *all* of it—is truth. Because of this, it will endure forever. Truth does not change or fade with time because Yahweh is the source of all truth, and *He* does not change or fade with time. We can be absolutely certain of the truth and rightness of the Scriptures because we know the One who authored them. As He is eternal and unchanging, so every one of His judgments will faithfully endure forever.

---

18. See Ephesians 2:12-13.

Application

- What are your initial thoughts and feelings toward those living in rebellion against God and His Word? Reflect on your heart posture and confess any pride that springs up. Ask the Holy Spirit to cultivate humble gratitude in your heart for the great mercy you have been shown, and pray for the salvation of the wicked as well.

- In what part of your life are you struggling with obedience? Dig down to the root of it—what area(s) of unbelief do you need to confess to the Lord today?

RESH | PRAYER

Heavenly Father,

Words cannot express my gratitude for the great mercy and endless grace You have shown me. I am deeply humbled to know that though I was dead in sin and living as Your enemy, You, through Christ, have paid the way for me to be in Your presence.

I confess my unbelief, and I ask You to help me believe to my very core that Your instructions are good because You are good. Thank You that I can know that the entirety of Your Word is trustworthy and true. Help me to live as though I believe it.

Amen.

Psalm 119:161–168

SIN & SHIN

161 Princes persecute me without cause,

but my heart stands in awe of your words.

162 I rejoice at your word

like one who finds great spoil.

163 I hate and abhor falsehood,

but I love your law.

164 Seven times a day I praise you

for your righteous rules.

165 Great peace have those who love your law;

nothing can make them stumble.

166 I hope for your salvation, O Lord,

and I do your commandments.

167 My soul keeps your testimonies;

I love them exceedingly.

168 I keep your precepts and testimonies,

for all my ways are before you.

Psalm 119:161-168

NOTES

Day 24

Psalm 119:161-168

1. What is the psalmist in awe of, and how does he respond to this feeling (vv. 161-162)?

2. What does the contrast of God's law with falsehood imply about the nature of God's law (v. 163)?

3. What does the psalmist mean when he says he praises the Lord seven times a day? Do you think he actually scheduled seven times during his days to stop and praise?

4. What is gained by those who love the law of the Lord (v. 165)?

5. Fill in the blanks about what the psalmist says he does in each of the following verses:
   - "...I ____ your commandments." (v. 166)
   - "My soul _____ your testimonies..." (v. 167)
   - "I _____ your precepts and testimonies..." (v. 168)

Devotional

The psalmist concludes his lengthy psalm by returning to several themes that he has previously spoken of, so we will refer back to many of the previous verses as we study the final two stanzas. The first concept is continued steadfastness amid frustrating or painful circumstances. We have walked with our psalmist through slander,[19] affliction,[20] persecution,[21] and entrapment.[22] The CSB's translation of verse 161 gives us insight into how he is able to withstand all of these things: rightly oriented fear. It says, "Princes have persecuted me without cause, but my heart fears only your word." His

---

19. See verses 23, 69, and 78.
20. See verses 50, 92, and 153.
21. See verses 51, 81, 86, 150, 157, and 161.
22. See verses 61, 85, 95, and 110.

healthy fear of the serious consequences of violating God's instructions gives our psalmist motivation to obey them. When we fear the Lord and His Word above all else, we can stand firm in the face of tribulation, distress, persecution, famine, nakedness, danger, or sword because we know that God is for us (see Rom. 8:31-35). Nothing in all of creation can separate us from the love of God in Christ Jesus (see Rom. 8:38-39), and He who is in us is greater than he who is in the world (see 1 Jn. 4:4).

The ESV's interpretation of this same phrase in verse 161 helps round out our understanding of what the psalmist is trying to convey. He not only fears the Lord but stands in awe of Him and, more specifically, His words. I think today, with hundreds of different translations, study Bibles, commentaries, and more at our fingertips, we miss the absolute wonder of the Scriptures. When we consider that we have the very words of Yahweh written down for us, it should bring us to our knees in worship, awe, gratitude, and joy.

The psalmist goes on to say that he hates and abhors falsehood. He contrasts it with God's law, and this contrast would only make sense with the assumption that God's law is truth. This has been directly stated in previous verses,[23] so again, we are revisiting and wrapping up some of the important themes of the psalm. The love of God's Word mentioned here is another incredibly strong theme that is both implied and directly mentioned many times.[24] His abiding love for the Scriptures brings forth praise from the psalmist for the righteousness of God's commands, which is yet another conviction he has continually mentioned.[25] In verse 164, he says that he praises the Lord seven times a day, which is not meant to be taken literally (though it is likely true). The number seven is used throughout the Bible to suggest completeness or thoroughness.[26] He is saying that he spontaneously and continuously praises the Lord throughout his days. The love of the psalmist for God's Word also brings him abundant peace, and this still holds true for us today. When we love the Scriptures, nothing can make us stumble because we stand on a firm foundation: the unwavering words of God Almighty. Love of God's instruction brings us peace because, through it, we learn God's character. If we are walking with Him, we have no need to worry or fear because we know that He is sovereign, good, and holy, and He deeply loves and cares for His children.

Our psalmist continues to wait with confident expectation for the salvation of the Lord. He is completely certain that God will keep His promises, and so he obeys. If we truly believe that the Lord will keep His word, faithful obedience is the only appropriate response. He delights in obeying because he deeply loves God and His commands. But he also obeys because he recognizes that the Lord sees all his ways. There is no hiding—no doing what's right in public and sinning in private—because everything is open and plain before the all-knowing One. Put another way, he cannot hide from God, but he has no reason to because he is living a life of obedience. Furthermore, when we love someone, we *want* to please them. It is plain to see that the writer of this psalm truly loves God and longs to please Him through obedience to His Word. Knowing that all his ways are before the Lord motivates the psalmist to

---

23. See verses 43, 142, 151, and 160.
24. See verses 47-48, 97, 113, 119, 127, 159, and 163.
25. See verses 7, 62, 75, 106, 123, 137, 144, and 160.
26. *NET Bible, Full Notes Edition* (Nashville, TN: Thomas Nelson, 2019), page 1046.

obey, as he desires to please the Lord with every moment, whether or not anyone else sees it. One commentator put it this way:

> "It is obedience that is the hallmark of love and it is by obedience we please the Lord."[27]

And Jesus Himself said it best:

> "If you love me, you will keep my commands."
> (John 14:15)

Application

- How often do you genuinely and spontaneously praise the Lord?

- What is your motivation for obedience to the Scriptures? Are you legalistic or fearful, or does your obedience spring from a heart that truly loves and longs to please your Savior?

27. J.A. Motyer, *The Psalms*, ed. D. A Carson et al., *New Bible Commentary: 21st Century Edition* (Downers Grove, IL: InterVarsity Press, 2010), pages 571-572.

SIN & SHIN | PRAYER

Dear Lord,

There are many things in this world that cause me to feel afraid, but I ask You to reorient my heart to fear You alone, for You are the only One worthy of fear.

I praise You for the truth and righteousness of Your Word. I ask You to help me love it more and more so that my heart may overflow with the peace that comes only from knowing You.

I pray that I would obey You not simply out of fear but from a heart longing to please the One I love. Keep my heart soft toward Your instruction.

Amen.

Psalm 119:169–176

TAW

169 Let my cry come before you, O Lord;

give me understanding according to your word!

170 Let my plea come before you;

deliver me according to your word.

171 My lips will pour forth praise,

for you teach me your statutes.

172 My tongue will sing of your word,

for all your commandments are right.

173 Let your hand be ready to help me,

for I have chosen your precepts.

174 I long for your salvation, O Lord,

and your law is my delight.

175 Let my soul live and praise you,

and let your rules help me.

176 I have gone astray like a lost sheep; seek your
servant,

for I do not forget your commandments.

Psalm 119:169-176

NOTES

Day 25

Psalm 119:169-176

1. What requests does the psalmist make of God in this stanza?

2. What parallels do you see in verses 171-172?

3. What reason does the psalmist give for the Lord to be ready to help him (v. 173)?

4. Why does the psalmist want to continue living (v. 175)?

5. Fill in the following blanks from verse 176:
   "I have _____ _____ like a _____ sheep; seek your _____,
   for I do not _____ your commandments."
   (Psalm 119:176, ESV)

Devotional

Yesterday's stanza ended with the psalmist remembering that all his ways are before the Lord (v. 168). This is incredible when you consider what he says next. After saying, "all my ways are before you," he asks the Lord to let his cries and pleas come before Him. It feels very bold, as if he is saying, "I know that You see and know all my ways, Lord, so why are You ignoring my cries? Pay attention to me!" We don't often pray with this level of honesty, do we? Yet the psalmist's cries are not rebellious. He wants to align his heart with God's and asks for understanding and deliverance to this end. He doesn't ask for anything outside of God's character or instruction, and therefore he is able to boldly approach the throne of grace.

134

The remainder of the psalm rings with a very strong theme of praise. Previously only mentioned four times in the entire psalm,[27] the psalmist speaks of praise three times just in this final stanza! As he wraps up this psalm about the word of God, he can't help but praise the Lord, the very source of these words that he so dearly loves. He specifically praises God for teaching him His statutes, which is something he has been asking God to do since he began writing this psalm.[28] This is something the Lord still does for His people today. He doesn't give us instructions and then leave us to figure them out on our own. Instead, He walks with us and guides us through His Word. Through His Spirit, He teaches us and opens our minds "that we might understand the things freely given us by God" (1 Cor. 2:12). This is a gift of grace that should stir our hearts to worship! The Hebrew word translated as "sings" in verse 172 literally means to answer or respond. The response of the psalmist to a greater understanding of the Word of God is a song of praise, and our response should be the same.

Next, the psalmist asks God for help, and he is confident that God will answer. Because he chooses to live in obedience, he can expect help from the Lord to continue obeying. Again, the Lord is so compassionate and gracious. He doesn't give us commands and then leave us to obey in our own strength. He instructs and then *enables* us to obey by His grace because He knows our frame (see Ps. 103:14). He knows that apart from Him, we can do nothing (see John 15:4-5). Our psalmist desires to live the rest of his life in worship. He knows that verbal praise is empty apart from obedience, but a life lived in faithfulness brings the Lord the utmost glory and honor.

Psalm 119 comes full circle at the end. The writer began the psalm by speaking of those who seek the Lord (v. 2), and then asked the Lord to keep him from wandering (v. 10). After so much time spent dwelling on the joy of walking in the ways of the Lord, the humility our psalmist displays at the end of the psalm is beautiful. He freely admits that he is still prone to wander. He needs the Lord to continue to seek his heart, even as he continues seeking the Lord. He longs to obey but is still at war with his sinful nature. He doesn't forget God's commands but needs God's help to obey them. It is not only at salvation that God pursues us; His goodness and mercy follow us all the days of our lives (see Ps. 23:6). As believers, when we stray like lost sheep, He continues to pursue us until we return in repentance to the Shepherd and Overseer of our souls (see 1 Pet. 2:24-25).

---

27. See verses 7, 62, 108, and 164.
28. See verses 12, 26, 29, 33, 64, 66, 68, 108, 124, and 135.

Application

- How honest are you when you pray? Do you try to sugarcoat your emotions before the Lord, or do you lay it all out plainly before Him? Remember that He already knows what you're feeling, and He is the only One who can guide your heart toward holiness.

- Though spiritually we have been made new, we will battle our sinful nature until our time on earth is done. Are you pridefully striving, trying to wrestle your flesh into submission, or are you humbly relying on the Holy Spirit to guide you into truth and obedience as you walk with the Lord?

TAW | PRAYER

Dear Lord,

Thank You for Your kindness and grace as You teach me the truth through Your Word. I ask that Your Holy Spirit would open my eyes to behold wondrous things from Your instruction (Psalm 119:18) and guide me into all truth (John 16:13).

May my life be one of true worship through faithful obedience for the rest of my days, to the glory of Your holy name.

Amen.

Day 26

Psalm 119

1. Take a few minutes to read through the entire psalm.

2. Take note of any additional insight or understanding the Holy Spirit gives as you read.

3. Spend a moment praising the Lord for the invaluable treasure He has given us in His Word.

Great peace have those who love your law; nothing can make them stumble.
PSALM 119:165

139

Note from the Author

What a journey it has been. What's next for you, friend? You've studied Psalm 119, but there are many more psalms and many other books in the Bible! Your work as a student of God's Word is not nearly finished. I encourage you to keep going! Choose a book of the Bible to study, and invite a friend to join you if you want someone to discuss it with and to hold you accountable for spending time with the Lord.

I hope you can utilize some of the tools you gained through this study to gain the confidence to begin studying the Bible on your own. You will never regret the time and effort spent seeking to know the Lord through His Word! Bible study is not always easy, but it is always worth it.

On the following page, I've compiled a list of some of my favorite Bible study resources, along with a short description of each to help you know which ones might be most useful to you. However, I never want you to feel like you have to buy anything in order to study God's Word! These are simply tools that have greatly aided me in my own understanding. I am praying for you as you continue growing in your Bible study skills and especially in your knowledge of our Lord!

All for the glory of God,

Traci Mae

Recommended Resources

- **Blue Letter Bible** (phone app or blueletterbible.org)
  Free access to Strong's Concordance as well as countless commentaries, sermon outlines, and other study tools.

- **Book Overviews**
  Several options are available, and each has its own unique advantages. Book overviews are helpful in understanding the genres, authorship, themes, and unique aspects of each book of the Bible. Two of my favorites are *Bible Study Guide* from Chasing Sacred and *The Bible Handbook* from The Daily Grace Co. If you prefer videos instead of books, BibleProject has an animated overview of each book of the Bible at bibleproject.com. Find the videos under the "Watch" tab.

- **IVP Bible Background Commentaries**
  With one book for the Old Testament and one for the New, these are incredibly helpful during the observation stage of study and are one of the first resources I reach for in my own study! They provide historical and cultural information about the time periods in which each book/passage of the Bible was written.

- **Bible Dictionary**
  Of course, there are too many Bible dictionary options available to list, but my personal favorite is the *Holman Illustrated Bible Dictionary*. It is written in a way that is very accessible and is also full of helpful illustrations and photos!

- **Color-Coding System**
  This is not everyone's cup of tea, but I find it immensely helpful to use a color coding system to draw out insights regarding structure, repeated words, and other aspects of the text. My top recommendation for this is, of course, what has become affectionately known as *The Bookmark* among some of my friends. It is available as a free digital download at everydayberean.com, or you can purchase physical bookmarks at everydayberean.etsy.com if you don't have a way to print your own.

- **Colored Pens/Pencils/Highlighters**
  Whether you use a color-coding system or not, it can be helpful to have a way to mark things that stand out to you. Find all of my favorite Bible-safe pens and highlighters at everydayberean.com!

- **Scripture Journals**
  These are available in both ESV and CSB, typically printed in one journal per book of the Bible (some of the smaller books are combined). If you don't want to fill up your nice Bible with notations, questions, etc., this resource is for you! Scripture journals are simply the text of the Scriptures printed with extra margin and spacing between lines, alongside full blank pages. These are fantastic if you're an avid note-taker like me!

Find more Bible study recommendations and resources at everydayberean.com!

141

everyday berean

The proceeds from the Everyday Berean Etsy shop
help fund the production & publication
of biblically sound devotionals, Bible studies,
& other Bible study tools.

Head to everydayberean.etsy.com
or scan the code below to support this ministry!

SCAN TO
SHOP

STAY IN TOUCH:

@everydayberean

everydayberean@gmail.com

everydayberean.etsy.com

everydayberean.substack.com